Xmas 2017

D1112009

for Vanessa

A THOUSAND DAYS IN BERLIN

TALES OF PROPERTY PIONEERING

from one Water
to another !

Andy

and the payer !

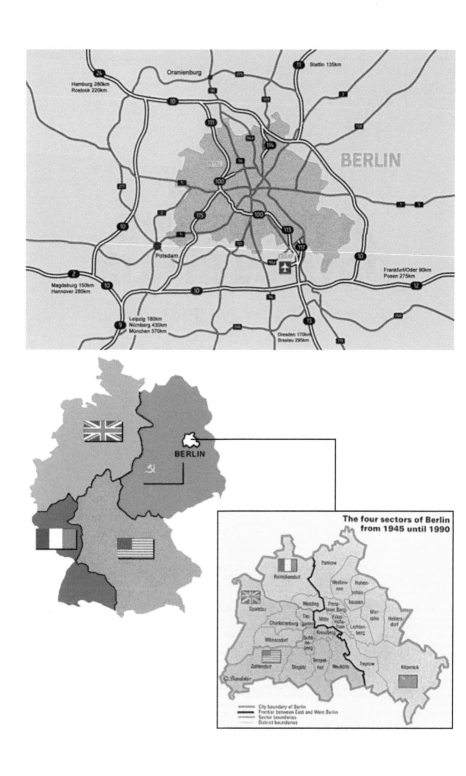

The four sectors of Berlin
from 1945 until 1990

City boundary of Berlin
Frontier between East and West Berlin
Sector boundaries
District boundaries

A THOUSAND DAYS IN BERLIN

TALES OF PROPERTY PIONEERING

By Andy Watson

PRINTED IN THE UNITED KINGDOM

Published through IngramSpark.

ISBN 9782956007401

Illustrations by Fabian Münster, Ottobrunn, Germany

Graphic design and composition by Raise, Kings Langley, UK

Printed by IngramSpark, Milton Keynes, UK

For Liz, who shared these unique pioneering days with me and for our three boys, Christopher, Ali & Jonny

The author in Berlin, 1992

Preface

F OR EXACTLY one thousand days I lived and worked in Berlin. That was almost 25 years ago. From 1 April 1992 until 31 December 1994 I was a resident and a young property professional in the newly reunified city. Those were exceptional times and it felt like a privilege just to be there. Knowing I was in the right place at the right time will still feel special in another 25 years.

Most of this book is not about today's Berlin, tomorrow's Berlin or the journey from the early 1990s. It's a personal story about *then* – a time when I rubbed shoulders with the genuine property pioneers and lived an intense experience.

My original plan was to write two or three chapters about Berlin in a book about a number of European cities. That changed as I started drafting tales of the vibrant place I had known so well in the early 1990s as a newly qualified chartered surveyor. Words flowed. The exercise revealed a rich seam of material, unique and personal to me. This exhilarating sense of ownership released a narrative voice which, I realised, was not present in other cities where I have never lived.

During its short but intense history Berlin has been long on energy and short on elegance. For the last hundred years the city has pulsated with energy, sometimes destructive, sometimes creative. Right now the growing city is, once again, a magnet for Europe's most animated and creative young people. It certainly energised me. Speaking with friends in Berlin who shared the experience of my thousand days felt like throwing open the doors of my own memory.

Timing is important. Received wisdom tells us that the three most important things in property are location, location and location. The late Chris Bull-Diamond, the man who gave me the chance to spend those thousand days in Berlin, used to say that the three most important things are actually timing, timing and timing. The timing for a Berlin book felt right in many ways.

A thousand days' residence in any city is sufficient time to really understand it. In the context of this book it was long enough to get under the skin of Berlin – but not too long. My (almost) three years there afforded me a viewpoint that was both objective and subjective. Moreover, it was not just any 1,000 days, but a pivotal period in the city's history. Like most of the residents of Berlin I knew at the time, I feel as if I packed more experience into those 33 months than in more 'normal' days before or since. We worked hard, played hard and put 60 seconds into every minute.

Most Europeans over the age of 40 can recall what they were doing on the November night when the Berlin Wall came down. Memory silts up slowly with the tide of time but for the residents of Berlin, the early 1990s still do not feel too distant. The people I interviewed for this book clearly remembered what happened in the intense years that followed and were keen to help shape the project. My most important source of inspiration, my creative muse, has been listening to these people recalling those times. As I was nearing completion of the text, Chris Bull-Diamond passed away suddenly. My old boss was an active supporter of, and contributor, to this book and the passing of a man so aware of the importance of timing reinforced my conviction that now is the time to record those thousand days in Berlin.

The timing seemed right in other ways. Berlin has recently become Germany's real estate city of choice and is regularly voted Europe's number one pick for property investors. After I left at the end of 1994, property values there continued to fall for almost 15 years, even though they were rising in most of Europe. It took a generation to heal Berlin's deep wounds and reverse the slow leakage of talented people, and to create a virtuous circle of optimism and rising values. Then, as I was gathering material for this book, the UK – surprisingly – voted to leave the EU. The uncertainty surrounding London's future position in Europe has further sharpened interest in Berlin from those who feel the time is right to live, work and invest there.

One last reflection on timing. For the moment, I believe the perspective and content of what follows is unique. Many words have been written about Berlin's upheaval in the 1990s, but not from the first-person perspective of a property professional who was at the centre of the action. The seat-of-the-pants property pioneers working in Berlin in those days were simply too busy trying to make money to have wasted their time writing it down.

So aside from a conviction that the time is right, what makes me qualified to write this book?

What I have written has been shaped by three personal passions: words, property and Germany. Unusually for a real estate professional, I have a literary background. In the late 1980s, I studied for a degree in German, which at Oxford University meant four years of old-fashioned literature in the German language. That formal training in decrypting Medieval High German helps explain my interest in the creative use of language and my strong interest in German culture.

Both academically and professionally, my most intense and instructive educational experience has been a German one. Prior to my transfer to Germany in early 1991, I had been what was euphemistically termed a 'non-cognate' graduate trainee with no background in real estate. 'Non-cognate' was a polite industry expression for knowing nothing. Worse than not knowing, I did not really care. Work just felt like duty calling – the road from studying for an arts degree to qualifying as a chartered surveyor seemed dull, fact-heavy and mechanical. After I arrived in Germany my passion for the property industry was sparked by the sudden and surprising historical revolution that Germans call '*die Wende*' (literally 'the turning').

'*Die Wende*' was my own turning point. Suddenly, in a German context, I found it stimulating to understand the workings of the built environment. In particular, it was easy to become passionate about reshaping the unique city of Berlin. That is what this book is about. I hope you, the reader, feel the same energy reading it as I have found in researching and writing it.

Maisons Laffitte, January 2017

Contents

Foreword

A Lifetime of Experiences in a Thousand Days

By Stuart Reid, Partner, Rockspring Berlin

I AM DELIGHTED that Andy asked me to write the foreword to his book, chronicling his personal experiences during our 'wild East' days. Berlin, the newly reborn city where Andy chose to live and work for 1,000 days, has now been my home for almost 10,000. In that time, I have seen a dynamic city come to terms with massive changes to its built environment.

Those early days now seem distant and quite impossible to believe. After the initial excitement, uncertainty, upheaval, growing pains and intense redevelopment, Berlin is now beginning to look and feel like a confident and proud gateway city. It looks (almost) polished and feels optimistic. Indeed, it is the very first multicultural and open German city, an international status which is a benefit to itself and to Germany as a whole.

My own move back from Japan in 1991 coincided with the start of what proved to be a prolonged property recession in the UK and USA. My former employer, Weatherall Green & Smith, offered me the opportunity to move to either Madrid (my wife's preference) or Berlin. Germany already boasted an attractive international investment market, but due to its unique (and I mean unique) history, only a very few local investors had been active in Berlin. It felt like a chance to be part of an exciting story. Andy, a trainee in Frankfurt in 1991, saw it the same way. He wanted action. As a young man, that is what he experienced – and by the bucketload. Andy joined our small office on Unter den Linden some 12 months after I had set it up.

Developers flooded to the city each week to reshape Berlin after 50 years as a subsidised backwater, a physical island landlocked in the middle of former East Germany. Professional advisors to these developers were scarce, creating a great opportunity. At the same time, nobody really knew what was going on. With the fall of the Wall, the dominant local west Berlin investors and developers, like the east Berliners, had lost their 'province'. The city government, town planning and local politics were all new. Most importantly, the city's geography was completely turned on its head as what had been out on a limb had shifted to the centre.

The pre-war heart of Berlin (Berlin-Mitte) was located in the former eastern sector. Mitte is now, once again, the CBD. Meanwhile, the former 'death strip' adjoining the Wall ran through the centre of the city. This land has now been rebuilt, echoing former street lines, as Potsdamer Platz and Leipziger Platz. In 1991 that geography was hard to envisage. Few passengers stopped at the former Lehrter railway station, an unimportant S-Bahn station just inside the west. Who could have known that Lehrter would be developed into Berlin Hauptbahnhof, the city's new main rail station? Since 2006, that main station has opened up a new central area and major business development site.

So all the cards were on the table and the players had arrived. The question was: 'what game are we playing?' There were no established track records, but there were new rules, new locations and new players. Real knowledge was rare and sometimes the best market information was gleaned by flying business class on the Monday morning BA flight from London to Berlin. Not the most detailed due diligence, but better than nothing. Enthusiasm and interest were strong but gossip was rife, real facts rare, locations changing and politics unknown.

Where else, as a young real estate professional, could one meet up with Stuart Lipton, Ronnie Lyon, Jerry Speyer, Peter Beckwith, Peter Munk, Godfrey Bradman and both Ronson cousins, Gerald and Howard? Where else were they willing to listen to your advice at such a young age? That advice was based on only six months of living in a city, but a city you knew better than they did. As Andy says, those pioneers of the property industry were starting to fill a blank page. Far be it from me to say that these were the days when "in the land of the blind, the one-eyed man is king", but it was not wide of the mark. It certainly was fun.

Andy mentions timing in his book and his own was pretty good, since he departed Berlin for Paris at the end of 1994 – shortly before Berlin's perfect storm of 1995/96. At that time of muted demand, the developer greyhounds all flew out of their traps to complete the first generation of office and retail properties. Rents collapsed as the hoped-for growth in population and office demand did not occur, leaving many to lose money. It took a long time for confidence to grow back.

In 2004, Mayor Klaus Wowereit described Berlin as "poor but sexy", and as recently as 2011, it was pretty difficult to sell property there. The city has now come of age and sits at the top of many investors' 'buy list'. Its rebuilding is mostly complete and the vast majority of infrastructure works have been finished (except, sadly, the new BER international airport where we still await an opening date). Population growth is strong and demand is booming from start-ups and the TMT sector. House prices, rents and values are soaring. Everyone wants a piece of the action, whether students visiting on Eurotrips, those seeking history and culture, international real estate investors or angel investors.

Andy has taken the time here to describe his first-hand adventures, which will never be repeated in Europe. I hope you enjoy reading these unique tales and take the time to visit our city. It has certainly moved on since those thousand pioneering days.

Stuart Reid
Partner, Rockspring Property Asset Management, Berlin
January 2017

Part One

1

THE COLD WAR AND THE HAND OF HISTORY

The four zones of occupation in post-war Berlin

BERLIN'S post-war history is a scientific experiment with fascinating implications for real estate. It works like this:

i) place one half of a devastated city under a totalitarian Communist regime and preserve under a bell jar;

ii) leave the other half of the city as a control experiment for 45 years;

iii) amplify and distort normal capitalist behaviours in the control experiment.

In my daily professional and personal life in Berlin, the heavy hand of history was everywhere – in the legacy of Communism, the cold war and, just occasionally, in the spooks of Nazism. In no European city is history more recent, more intense and more tangible than in Berlin. In 1992, you could touch it, feel it, see it. Sometimes, you could even smell the history.

In many major cities in Europe, the mass destruction between 1939 and

1945 has left its mark on the built environment. The reconstruction of Frankfurt, Munich, Milan, London, Warsaw and Rotterdam can be viewed in 1950s black and white newsreels. The history which shaped Berlin's skyline is so recent and so immediate that it can be accessed in colour on *YouTube*.

In May 1988, I first felt the weight of history 'live' as a student visiting East Berlin with 50 of my peers from around the world. In retrospect, the experience was a life changer. Twice in the course of that short week I saw student friends test East German border guards. Both times, at Checkpoint Alpha and Checkpoint Charlie, they came away chastened young men. The officials of the *Deutsche Demokratische Republik* (DDR) had sharp teeth and obeyed a very different rulebook.

The author at Checkpoint Charlie (American Zone) May 1988

When our coach entered East Germany at Checkpoint Alpha, a grey-uniformed East German woman boarded to check passports. Never had I seen passports so thoroughly verified with so many odd questions. Earlier, as we frolicked over a few cold beers in the sun, Simon, a goth from Birmingham University, had decided it would be funny to place a Euro 88 sticker of the

3

blond West German striker Jürgen Klinsmann over the top of his official passport picture. The stern and stocky passport checker in grey did not do humour: "*Aber Sie sind nicht Jürgen Klinsmann*" ("But you're not Jürgen Klinsmann"). In her world his student prank was just condescending and subversive, and she manhandled him off the bus in a muscular way.

As a result, Simon's friends in the hot vehicle all had to wait for two hours while he was interrogated in a Portakabin. The black-clad young goth was a friendless man when he returned – in fact, most of the time the guards had just left him to sweat in a dark room in his black leathers. Our coach was finally allowed to proceed along East Germany's eerie motorway corridor to the oasis of West Berlin. On the bus, quiet anxiety had replaced student euphoria and our cheerful moment of camaraderie in the sun had been squashed by the heavy hand of the DDR.

Stefan, an exchange student from the USA, came off worse than Simon the goth. Tourists entering the East were obliged to exchange DM 25 at the DDR's official rate of 1:1. The unofficial rate was 5:1 or 6:1. We were warned of the dire consequences of exchanging money at those attractive-looking

rates on the black market. Fearless Stefan chose to ignore those explicit warnings and, once through the checkpoint, he jumped on a tram to spend the day on his own exploring what he described as "the real East Germany". In that real East, Stef found a buyer for his Deutschmarks quite easily. For DM 50 cash (€26) he was given 300 Ostmarks and went shopping in a local *Kaufhaus*. He purchased the single most expensive item in the store – a thick black leather coat – for just under 200 Ostmarks.

Unter den Linden – May 1988

4

Before passing back through Checkpoint Charlie just before midnight, the tall and confident Californian jettisoned both the receipt for the coat and his many excess Ostmarks. Unfortunately for Stef, his new garment was an instant giveaway to the border guards. Only a handful of those distinctive luxury leather coats were available in the whole of East Berlin. With so few shops in the East, the guards knew the exact store where it must have been purchased as well as the exact price – which was eight times the maximum amount of currency that tourists were legally allowed to carry.

Stef was detained, taken out the back of the checkpoint, stripped, searched and given a sharp lesson about adhering to local rules. We were all worried when he did not appear at our West Berlin hotel, especially as we were aware of Stef's risky shopping intentions. He got back at five in the morning, a smaller man, having left the leather coat in the East and been 'let off' with a cash fine. Later in the week, most of our party went across to fascinating East Berlin for a second day, Stefan did not join us.

Walking down Unter den Linden, we saw the heavy grey military uniform again – this time combined with threatening jackboots in one of the regular parades staged by Erich Honecker to show off the DDR's military strength. Shortly afterwards, I briefly mislaid my passport in a grisly café near Alexanderplatz. I traced where I had left it and ran to where the bag containing the passport should have been. When I arrived, the bag had gone. I froze. Two long minutes later, the old café owner returned it with the comment that I should really be more careful. With the experiences of Simon and Stefan fresh in the mind, my head was spinning with the consequences of being trapped in the oppressive East.

These were formative moments in my young student life. When I returned four years later as a trainee property professional, that week's excursion proved a big advantage in helping me understand the people and property of the city. I was surrounded by the legacy of the former DDR I had tasted in May 1988. Unusually for the time, although I lived in the West, I worked on Unter den Linden in east Berlin, the *avenue des Champs Elysées* of the DDR, very close to the spot where I had seen the goose-stepping soldiers. My office building was an interesting microcosm of daily life under the hand of Communism.

Unter den Linden Number Twelve (UDL12) was a handsome bite-sized piece of real estate. Built just before the First World War, the well-proportioned, five-level property had a sandstone facade, style and presence.

Unter den Linden 12 – 1992

The location needs cultural context for today's reader. For 60 million West Germans, Unter den Linden was a place in a fairy tale, lost for two generations to Honecker's parades. Being there felt rather like having slipped through the wardrobe in CS Lewis' *Narnia*. In that neglected kingdom where few buildings were suitable for office occupation, I was very lucky to work in the equivalent of a castle. The location of the castle was 100% prime, next to the corner of two mythical addresses – Unter den Linden and Friedrichstraße.

Clean title was still very rare and most ownership disputes had to be processed by the *Treuhandanstalt* (THA) – the organisation dealing with restitutions to those dispossessed either by Nazi Germany or by the Soviet Union in 1945. Our little UDL 12 building had an uncontested and unusually clean ownership, traceable to the inheritors of Graf von Ballestrem, a noble family from Silesia, a region now mostly in Poland. Title was swiftly returned to the family by the THA, the building was lightly refurbished and let to businesses which wanted to get a toehold in the Berlin market. They snapped up the small 250 m² office floors at a world-class address with emotional clout for Germans.

6

The office tenants were a fair sample of 1992 business in Berlin and included my company, property advisors Weatherall Green and Smith; an American property developer (Tishman Speyer); and architects (our subtenant RKW). Short leases for periods of 24 or 36 months were agreed at DM 90 per m² per month (about €600 per m² per annum at today's values) – the same levels as for the best space in the best locations in Frankfurt and west Berlin.

After moving to Paris some years later, I would realise that those office suites had a 'Haussmannian' feel, with very high ceilings that made them comfortably cool in the hot central European summers. From my desk, the views over the many development sites along Friedrichstraße were memorable. I parked my small company car in a murky overground multi-storey bunker – but in a prime location. Public transport was the overland S-Bahn at the very big Friedrichstraße station (which the DDR authorities famously labelled "the last station in the democratic sector").

East Berlin at lunchtime was a culinary desert, even at the main hub around Unter den Linden. The neighbouring *Staatsbibliothek* (public library) canteen was open for pickled gherkins, deep-fried meatballs, stodgy potato salad, black dry bread and a token piece of wilting lettuce. Day after day, that was the menu. The buffet of the new hotel Hilton on Gendarmenmarkt was almost the only place in walking distance serving food that would not fur the arteries. Months later, TGI Friday opened a branch close to the cathedral. It sold fresh fruit salad and felt like a great option.

Unter den Linden 12 was a property with a past. Its most recent occupier had been the 'committee for Anti-Fascist activities', which, in practice, meant the secret service. The *Staatssicherheitsdienst* directly employed 100,000 staff and indirectly employed a further 200,000 informants, an extraordinarily high number in a country of 16 million people. It was no surprise to learn that the Stasi had made use of UDL 12, nestled as it was between embassies of both Eastern and Western countries and close to the new Grand Hotel, where foreign visitors could be observed.

The building itself illustrated the colossal inconsistencies of the Communist system. To the front, a thin sandstone facade of glory overlooked the Unter den Linden parade ground of the DDR, the prestige address in East Germany. Easterners talked about the "Honecker Line": if the leader could see a property out of the window of his Volvo at parade time then the building had to *appear* to be in order. Behind that – or above that – nobody cared. Two streets further back were buildings that had not seen paint since the 1930s.

Behind the attractive facade, however, our building still had the deep and visible scars of the battle for Berlin. Large bullet holes from April 1945 were visible from our boardroom table overlooking the *Hinterhof*, or rear courtyard. It was not just the odd pockmark or graze: multiple bullets from what I imagined was a machine-gun had shredded away huge chunks of masonry. The legacies of long years of subsequent Communist neglect were also visible, with downpipes wrapped tight in old rags, stained the colour of tea by a slow drip. The new owner's recent upgrade had not extended to the rear of our building.

In taking a pre-lease, the main risk my company faced was a potential lack of telephone lines in the days when mobile phones (outside Asia) were the size of briefcases and the preserve of the wealthy. Never mind mobiles, when the Wall came down in late 1989, only one East German

Central East Berlin 1992 – Two streets back from Unter den Linden, buildings had not seen paint since the 1930s (note the recently removed hammer and compass – the DDR's national emblem)

in fourteen had a home telephone. In 1992 there was, of course, no SMS or email, so without office telephones we would have been completely out of touch. Today that sort of wi-fi-free peace can only be found in the African bush but it is worth recalling that being *incommunicado* did not feel unusual or too worrying at the time.

Our phone dilemma was solved in a surprising way. During the technical refurbishment of the building dozens of phone lines were uncovered in the basement – concealed beneath several hammer and compass DDR flags and giant cartoon posters of jaunty square-jawed socialist workers. Above the neatly drilled holes in the wall were neatly typewritten labels reading: "USA in", "USA out", "GB in", "GB out", "France in", "France out". The previous occupiers had been listening in to telephone conversations in the nearby western embassies. As with the Nazis before them, the German passion for *Ordnung* made it easy to trace the Stasi's activities.

Those phone lines, however, proved unreliable. Someone speaking in London could sound as if they were talking in the room next door, but a speaker in the East – just 400 metres away – could sound so distorted they might have been using a child's walkie-talkie. Sometimes a digger on one of the many building sites would cut a wire and the phone service would go dead. In those enforced communication downtimes I walked Berlin's streets, compiling lists of tenants from buildings by hand for old-style mailshots notifying them of our offices to let. These old ways still worked well too.

In retrospect, with the 'Wall in the mind' still very high, it was forward-looking of Weatheralls to set up in the former East. Over 90 % of Berlin

Corner Unter den Linden / Friedrichstraße in 1985 (IHZ tower is clearly visible to the right).
(photo: Gerd Danigel)

ex Stasi HQ – Berlin Lichtenberg 1992

businesspeople still chose to be based in the former West. For a property agent, clean ownership was important to generate fee income from transacting land and buildings. In 1992, that meant they mostly favoured west Berlin.

From our UDL 12 base, I was able to visit masses of disused real estate in the East for our clients. In 1989 about a third of flats in Berlin-Mitte were already vacant, as the Communist regime had been actively pursuing a policy of emptying flats to house the 'Happy Few' of the Party. By 1992, as 100,000 ownership claims poured in to block occupation, large slices of east Berlin felt really empty. Buildings were often in bizarre and disconnected locations, whilst land was often immensely polluted. The recurring questions for us as advisors were how buildings could most profitably be decontaminated and redeveloped and where, in a polycentric city, a prime location would emerge in the long term.

One memorable 'hand of history' moment was inspecting the vacant Stasi HQ in the Lichtenberg district, just off Karl-Marx-Allee. Even on a sunny day, this grand alley of rectangular concrete usually felt desolate. When the wind blew, the too-wide boulevard could feel desperate.

The public space was designed by Josef Stalin's town planners who, like the Stasi, sought to make the people feel small and disconnected. The acrid smell of asbestos dust was a powerful olfactory experience. The long, wide, murky corridors were served by a dark and strange Paternoster chain lift. Timing was key in that wood panelled elevator. Once upon a time the Stasi staff (perhaps filing reports from anti-fascist listeners in UDL 12) would have needed to hop in and out at just the right time or they'd go over the top or under the bottom of the lift shaft. No more than two people were allowed in a cabin at any one time. In my mind, the gentle disorientation of the continuous cycle was like one of the main goals of the Stasi: *Zersetzung* or mental disintegration.

In the centre of east Berlin I touched a less well-known commercial side of Communism. The *Internationales Handelszentrum* (IHZ) at Friedrichstraße 95 was the World Trade Center of East Germany, built to prove that trade was possible with partners outside the DDR. Office rents were even paid in US dollars. After reunification, the many embassies and consulates in the IHZ found themselves surplus to requirements for the

simple reason that East Germany had ceased to exist. They were replaced by other service providers such as my client, the lawyers Bruckhaus Westermann Stege, who instructed my company to sublet 800 m² – half of one floor.

The IHZ was built by a Japanese contractor, Kajima, which had once employed our office manager from East Berlin. She knew the drill in the IHZ, where the standard operating procedure had been to provide information to the authorities about the international tenants.

Ex Stasi HQ – Paternoster Lift

In its former life the 93-metre-high building possessed a unique selling point in the East: the offices looked down into the decadent West, so the tenants needed close monitoring in case they got ideas. The hand of the Stasi and its collaborators reached everywhere.

Berlin was the front line in the Cold War. I got a breath of that *kalter Krieg* in a mixed-use commercial building on Uhlandstraße in the centre of the West. Far beneath the office floors and a strange shopping gallery, I visited the *Atomschutzbunker*, a 1970s precaution in the event of nuclear war. The bunker was one of sixteen in the West and housed thousands of mini flip-up camp beds. These shelters had room for less than one in a hundred of the West Berlin population, on a strict first-come, first-served basis. Behind the airlocks, the oxygen was thin. After just half an hour inside the bunker, the dim blue lighting was playing tricks on my mind. The bunker, a pure propaganda stunt, was functionally useless.

The *Besatzungsmächte* (Occupational Forces) provided me with a more cheerful experience of the legacy of the Cold War. In the British sector, the Officers' Club was able to satisfy my twin addictions of cricket and history. I played in the Berlin Cricket League comprising West Indians, Indians, Pakistanis and a mixed-origin Commonwealth team. It was surreal to take guard on the cricket square close to Hitler's iconic Olympic Stadium. It was a world of privilege where the outfield's soft English-style lawn (most unusual in Germany) had been neatly mown in stripes and the batting surface looked as if it had been trimmed with nail scissors. The Allied Occupational Forces, the Americans, British and French stayed in Berlin for 50 years and left at almost the same time as me, in early 1995.

Sometimes the hand of history in Berlin stretched all the way back to the Nazi era. For obvious reasons, Nazism was harder to find in East Berlin, as the Soviets had been thorough in eradicating any lingering traces. The palace of the Hohenzollern monarch, for example, was dynamited to create the DDR's *Volkspalast* (itself recently demolished by Angela Merkel's government to rebuild the former *Schloss*). Whereas in Munich, the scale, volume and grandeur of Third Reich architecture can still be imagined today, emblems of

Nazism in Berlin were almost totally obliterated in the land battle of April 1945. Hitler's bunker was left buried under prefabricated concrete flats reserved for DDR icons such as Olympic ice skating champion Katarina Witt. One rare exception which remained largely intact was Göring's Luftwaffe HQ building which the DDR used as its *Haus der Ministerien* (House of Ministries). Curiously, that building on Wilhelmstraße is now Frau Merkel's national tax office HQ.

In my professional life as an office leasing agent, I occasionally touched the ghost of Nazism. In a little co-ownership property on the main Bundesallee, a bread-and-butter location in west Berlin, my company was offering 350 m² of vacant ground-floor offices – a deep, dark space which felt like a school but without the vibrant energy of the pupils. It was hard to identify the reason, but the space had poor karma and turned out to be unlettable at any price. I managed to get people there for viewings because, on paper, it looked cheap for the location – but up close, the aura always proved a turn-off. After a year, we dropped the instruction and I learned from the landlord that the Gestapo had occupied the property in the 1940s. For years afterwards, that information left me feeling curiously uncomfortable.

In all of these stories, the reader will see that history greatly influenced my thousand days in Berlin, for the simple reason that the city's recent history was shaped by dark and desperate behaviour – whether in the Nazi or Cold War period. Nevertheless, life in Berlin at the time did not feel nearly as sombre as all this might make it sound. The reader will see in the following chapters that the hope, expectations and energy of the new pioneering spirit were more powerful than the heavy hand of history.

2 LIVING IN BIPOLAR BERLIN – LIBERAL CULTURE, HARD-CORE CITY

BETWEEN 1961 and 1989, both Berlins had been in cultural overdrive as they strove to prove the superiority of their respective systems. Post-*Wende*, the cup of culture continued to overflow. For a newcomer like me, there were not one but two cities to explore. This chapter is about the rich cultural scene in the reunified city and the unique behaviour of Berliners out of the office.

The fascinating history of Berlin had actively shaped its compelling characters, and not always in a likeable fashion. The social context of Berlin was complex and prickly as the people of East and West were wary of each other and outsiders were not always welcome. As a Germanophile, I often rationalised a disconnect in my mind between 'The Germans' and individual Germans. Happily, we made many long-lasting German friends and 22 years after leaving the country we are still in contact with generous and inspiring

German individuals – as well as their children. Collectively, however, 'The Germans' in Berlin could come over as intimidating, in West and East alike.

Playtime – Liz Watson,
Alexanderplatz 1993

East Berlin's social atmosphere was especially intriguing. Getting close to daily life in the former DDR felt like bouncing between philanthropism and voyeurism. My colleague Regina's small apartment in Pankow was a snapshot of that daily life in the east. The windows did not fit inside their plastic frames and the cold air came through her thin and poorly insulated walls. The electric heating in the flat produced the same uncomfortable hot flush sensation as in the former DDR's clanky old trams. Regina had grown accustomed to being cold in the course of 30 years in the East and took a cold shower every morning because, she felt, it was good for her health.

The only place to go out to eat near her flat was a basic pizzeria. Europe nowadays is swamped with humdrum pizza restaurants, but in Pankow in early 1992 it felt like a sprinkling of colour in a grey world. Regina explained that in former times, ordering a humble 'Hawaii Toast' seemed like a breath of exoticism, as pineapples imported from faraway Cuba made people dream of impossible excursions to escape the dull *Alltag*. A Pizza Hawaii was even more exotic than toast and pineapples. When we finished our dinner, I paid the bill by visa card. Even west Berlin was (and still is) a cash-first culture, so my TSB card raised eyebrows in the East. The staff unwrapped their new credit card machine for one of their first plastic transactions. Like the pineapples and the décor of the pizzeria itself, paying by card was like black magic for Regina's young daughter Elsi, who remembered me for a time afterwards as the man who bought dinner without using money.

Like stepping back in time to 1939 – Prenzlauer Berg in 1989 *(photo: Gerd Danigel)*

Not many of our recently arrived international friends had the courage to join Regina in the East. The pioneer was my squash partner, Peter Storey of Barclays Bank, who leased a flat in Prenzlauer Berg, a cultural step further out from Pankow. Today, many inhabitants of 'Prenzlberg' are said to be from wealthy Stuttgart and the vibe of the multicultural bars and cafés beneath the arches of Eberswalder Straße even has a breath of stylish central Paris. In 1993, however, visiting Peter felt like stepping back in time to 1939. We all admired his spirit of adventure and asked, solicitously, what it was like, as if he'd been on holiday in Cuba.

My fiancée Liz came to visit *bei Regina* in Pankow in a cold, snowy February. My dream of an exciting life in the reunified Berlin nearly ended there and then. As we headed back through the East, our screeching tramway carriage was, by turns, hot and cold, the dirty snow lay brown on the broken pavements and the grey sky was low and heavy with *Schneeregen* (sleet). The major building works to relay Pankow's drains obscured the rare shops. Those shops, in turn, were mostly obscured by graffitied shutters. In the face of all that, Liz, understandably, said she could not live in Berlin. I promised that west Berlin would be a softer experience, especially in spring. Happily for this book, Liz swiftly came around to the idea.

The extreme weather had a big influence on the ambiance in Berlin. The central European climate amplified both the existing mood and the feel of the built environment. In the spring, sunny days made you look up – cheerfully – at the abundant green space, the beer gardens, the lakes and the parks. In winter, the short, dark days made you look down – at the rectangular concrete buildings, scrubland and ugly graffiti. Summer (very hot) and winter (very cold) were punctuated by a brief spring and a quick autumn. The grim winter skies felt as if they were sitting on one's shoulders, especially when returning to Berlin from Christmas holidays in the UK. Few of our international friends chose to stay in the city for the festive season.

Our thousand days were a time when Berliners were rediscovering freedom of travel. This was particularly true of the trains. Between 1991 and 1995, underground train stations that had been walled up since 1961 were constantly being reopened, uncovering peeling poster advertisements. The station walls had the look and feel of TV's *Mad Men* era, with funky retro art selling products from the early 1960s.

The former DDR's maps of the city presented the West as virgin white space marked as *terra incognita*. No underground lines were marked there. However, western passenger trains had been running underneath a part of the Russian sector

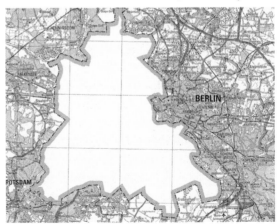

The DDR's map of Berlin and Potsdam in 1988

without its citizens knowing it. One of the strangest legacies we saw were the *Geisterbahnhöfe* or ghost stations which resulted from those secret journeys beneath Berlin Mitte. DDR guards had monitored Western trains rolling through a handful of boarded up and darkened stations without stopping and some guards had even jumped on the moving trains in an attempt to escape. As a result, this important duty was later entrusted only to 'reliable guards'.

Post-*Wende*, the East-West *Stadtschnellbahn* (known universally as S-Bahn) line was the rapid transport spine of the reunified city, in the same

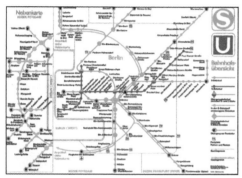

DDR Berlin metro map – which airbrushed out West Berlin to make a circle line to Potsdam!

way that the RER A line is the 'backbone' of Paris. The main difference is that almost all of the Berlin S-Bahn runs overland and passengers could actually see the changing aspect of the city. The visual treat of the S-Bahn line was the subject of a unique TV programme in the early 1990s. Starting from midnight, local television would show a real-time loop of an S-Bahn carriage trundling from east to west and back again. The unedited TV footage lasted about 75 minutes and ended near the beach, in the western station of Wannsee. Then it chugged back east towards *Endstation Bernau*. In the stations the noise of the old diesel engines would cut out and passengers would get on and off before the train trundled onwards. After a few late-night beers this peculiar programme became compelling midnight viewing for me (a colleague of Liz's even gave me the S-Bahn video as a leaving present). The show ran on Berlin television for years so it must have had an audience. The point, I guess, was that for 28 years both Easterners and Westerners had been unable to see the other side of the Wall, so local TV's late-night loop satisfied a pent-up curiosity.

Trams were discontinued in West Berlin in the 1960s, but they remained a very important mode of transport in the East. The rolling stock looked and felt ancient, like Milan's famous 'wooden leg' steam-powered trams or the old-style tramcars in Prague. They were also quite an assault on the senses. The seating area smelled smoky, oily and fuggy and managed to sound both high-pitched screechy and low-pitched clanky. The carriage usually felt either very hot – especially when sitting on top of the electric heater under the varnished wooden bench slats – or very cold, in most of the rest of the carriage.

Many of the palpable tensions between East and West came to the surface on Berlin's reunified roads. Driving was a tense adventure, even as a taxi passenger. I have driven in challenging Paris traffic for over 20 years and got used to the anarchic roads in Italy, but Berlin drivers were aggressive in a different and very personal way. I still remember clearly their characteristic gesture of a tap on the forehead, an accusatory roll of the eyes and three quick waves of the hand across the face.

"Fraser Denton of MDA Bysh acquired something more imposing"
A Russian BTR-40 armoured personnel carrier in the field

Some of my clients and friends experimented with exotic vehicles from the former East. Stephen Brook of Norwich Union bought a cheap Trabant to drive back to Norwich via Bremerhaven. The Trabi broke down near a tunnel and he abandoned it on the motorway, having failed to persuade a west

German garage owner to buy it off him. Fraser Denton of MDA Bysh acquired something more imposing: a part share in a Russian armoured car. He and a friend had attended a Russian army auction of military hardware and came away with a meaty BTR-40 armoured personnel vehicle. For a few months he felt very cool rolling up to parties in wild Kreuzberg in a vehicle made for battle. Like the plastic Trabant, however, the armoured car had a short shelf life. The common thread was that there were no spare parts available for either vehicle when things went wrong.

With the exception of the odd armoured car, the rules of the road seemed important to Berliners – as did parking straight. In the car park of a west Berlin supermarket, my wife and I were given a long moral sermon when our parked Honda missed the perpendicular by less than five degrees.

Friedenau roofscape – the view from our apartment in 1992

Such sermons were frequent at pedestrian lights. Walking across an empty road against a red signal would trigger tut-tutting lectures about the need to set good examples to children. Interestingly, the former DDR's perky *Ampelmann* has become an icon of today's Berlin. The *Ampelmann* is the famous red/green character on pedestrian lights wearing a wide-brimmed hat at a jaunty angle. It feels somehow significant that a symbol of traffic control should have such a prominent role. On the road, rules ruled, even in liberal, free-thinking Berlin.

We came to learn that this extreme respect for the rules was conditioned by the BGB, the *Bürgerliches Gesetzbuch* (civil code) which set out the rules of behaviour to Germans. It regulated many things in life, including how to correctly cross the road, where and how to shop and the (very restrictive) hours for mowing the lawn. The BGB code was behaviour by numbers.

The culture of denouncing one's neighbours had a long and dark history in Berlin and seemed to run deep. This was not just true in the East – many of our Western neighbours in Wilhelmshöher Straße, Friedenau still seemed hostile and suspicious. In their eyes we were '*schicki mickis*' – Flash Harrys who could afford to pay twice their low historic rents, and foreign ones to boot. The landlord's recent extension in the roof had made a lot of noise and dust and we were the obvious people to blame as we now occupied that nicely developed roof space (but with no lift and 104 steps to climb to the top). Liz and I were the face of change for a group of people who were struggling to cope with change.

Anonymous handwritten notes would appear on our car windscreen and in our letterbox. The messages were petty – pointing out, for example, how untidily we parked our small car in the little tarmacked *Hinterhof*. We were accused of making the *Hinterhof's* old metal chain "dirty" by driving over it, rather than getting out of the car and pulling it to one side. Judging by the twitching net curtain in his ground-floor flat, the old Hausmeister was the likely ringleader of the handwritten-note campaign. Gradually the notes lost their sting and became part of life, but we had come to understand the paranoia of being observed which Berliners were familiar with. If these messages had been pasted in cut-out newsprint letters, they could scarcely have been creepier. This was truly the worst of what I thought of as 'The Germans' in the negative collective sense.

Notwithstanding this narrow-minded behaviour, Berlin was full of open-minded and creative individuals. The liberal culture of David Bowie and the Kit Kat Club of *Cabaret* was naturally at odds with the book burnings and suppression of individuality by totalitarian regimes. In 1992, the city remained home to draft dodgers, artists, performers, poets, musicians and squatters with a free-thinking cultural heritage which went back to the 1920s and '30s. In their different ways, both Nazi and Communist governments had wanted to appear creative and show Berliners they were not philistines.

In a parallel universe to the property world, we found lots of informal cultural opportunities. My friend and former tutorial partner Anne had left Oxford with a first in Philosophy and German (she had kindly let me borrow some of her brilliant literature essays) to settle in Berlin immediately after university. Through Anne we got to know Andreas and Natascha, both young actors who embodied the Berlin which mayor Klaus Wowereit would later famously describe as "*arm aber sexy*" (poor but sexy). Like the diminutive and super-intelligent Anne, they had nothing to do with making money or the real estate industry. All three were beautiful innocents, unspoiled by commerce. One evening, Natascha and Andreas invited us to a shed in a family allotment garden for a cake to celebrate the coming of autumn. They took us to a performance of Shakespeare's *Midsummer Night's Dream*, in German, at a local school. They were the beating heart of creative Berlin.

Cabaret provided the most powerful and chilling piece of theatre I have ever seen. The Oscar-winning 1972 film has always been a personal favourite, but this 1992 production was special for being staged both in the German language and live in the city where Christopher Isherwood's original books were set. As film and theatre fans will know, the break for the interval is set up by the engaging blond boy singing tunefully in the beer garden. As the child in the khaki uniform of the *Hitler Jugend* sings louder, the watching crowd swells to sing the rousing National Socialist hymn '*der morgige Tag ist mein*' (Tomorrow Belongs to Me). In that production at Theater des Westens, the first half climaxed with the entire beer-garden crowd giving the Hitler salute and revealing swastikas from beneath their jackets. In the still deeply-wounded city of Berlin, it was compelling to witness this stage version. Over a glass of Sekt in the red-carpeted bar, no one tried to speak during the interval. The performance was so strong that we all felt as if we had just touched history.

Cabaret was one of two very intense cultural moments that book-ended our time in Berlin, the other being *Schindler's List* in the cinema. After we saw Spielberg's powerful film, the public filed out and walked home in silence. Just as in the half-time interval at *Cabaret*, the film felt so recent and so raw that no-one could speak. Once again the power of art and history was beyond words.

Between these two experiences at the beginning and end of our stay, we grabbed the chance to see performances in both Berlins. We saw Wagner's *Tannhäuser* in the Opera House (the grander Eastern venue) and Elton John in the atmospheric outdoor *Waldbühne*, near the Olympic Stadium. We regularly went to east Berlin's *Chamäleon* theatre to see world-class mime artists perform mesmerising routines such as the sliding escalator walk of the smiling Japanese acrobat.

Berlin had a big reputation as a party city and it did not disappoint. In both East and West, there were regular places to meet and party all night. In the East, brickies from Dublin and Cork would gather every Friday night in the Oscar Wilde Irish pub on Friedrichstraße. The construction boom meant

Party Central west – The Healey and Baker team in front of the Irish Harp Pub

they could always find *ad hoc* work at the Oscar Wilde. In the west, the Irish Harp pub was also a favourite venue for property people, especially my own chartered surveyor community in suits and early-1990s silk ties. We sang along to feelgood anthems like *Take Me Home, Country Roads*. There was a unique team spirit among the newbie property people as we explored the singing and dancing options. Gooch & Wagstaff, King & Co, Richard Ellis, Vail Williams, MDA Bysh and EC Harris would drink and chat together. In those opaque days before social media, the Irish pubs functioned as the information superhighway for the internationals. We were a Facebook group with Guinness. The small community of project managers (known as 'the anoraks') even managed the trick of becoming regulars in both these Irish pubs, with their very distinct clienteles.

Berlin by night had a reputation for being steamy and edgy. The term "Night Club" was deliberately ambiguous in Berlin – yet the infamous clubs did not somehow come across as particularly seedy: Liz and her colleague Cordelia often came along. The Mon Chéri club was well known with the Occupational Forces of the British Army for its prime attraction: The Bath Show. Friends in Her Majesty's Forces told of how a vast foaming bathtub

Party Central east – The garden of the Tacheles Squat, Oranienburger Straße 1992

would be lowered down from the ceiling and young women wearing only bubble bath would pull in a squaddie from the audience for a scrub up. 'Good Clean Fun', as the advertisement said in English. These clubs were more like Disneyland than their sweaty cousins in places like Pigalle. In the nearby Thai transsexual club, the girls were actually boys. The tell-tale sign of a ladyboy (or so it was explained) was the prominent Adam's apple.

In the East, close to the historic city centre, the hub of the Berlin party scene was the *Scheunenviertel*, the Jewish Quarter around Oranienburger Straße. The strip of bars here was a mix of improvised shelters such as the oddly-named *Obst und Gemüse* (literally 'fruit and vegetables') and occupied squats such as *Kunsthaus Tacheles*. This building, once the wartime HQ of the SS, now curiously sported a Russian MIG fighter in the back garden. There was music and there were artists performing. There were substances. There was a breath of something novel and unique in the East. Freedom and anarchy. All along Oranienburger Straße, the new capitalism had attracted some of the top sex workers from the Warsaw Pact countries – with their long white leather boots and matching white-feathered jackets. In full view of huge drinking

Obst und Gemüse Bar, Oranienburger Straße 1992 (photo: Berliner Morgenpost 'Wonderland')

25

crowds, the women in white bargained calmly with clients in Mercedes and clients in Skodas and Ladas. Sparks flew on the overhead tramlines. Fire-eaters appeared in scrubland between buildings. It was like an urban Mad Max scene. Somewhere in our thousand days, this unique historical phenomenon changed in character. The most tangible measure of that change was when the squatters started charging entry. *Eintritt* was only one Deutschmark but it felt like a pivotal moment: anarchy was getting organised.

If the leisure opportunities in Berlin by night were extensive, Berlin by day had natural advantages. Berlin is the most spread-out capital city in Europe; flying in, the aerial view is of a strikingly green land mass with plenty of water. Berlin was at its finest in spring and summer when the lakes and parks were green and friendly. Sport was widely available: football, swimming, hockey, softball, badminton, squash: even cricket. At the Alt-Lietzow squash club, we got to share mixed gender showers with swimmers from the pool. That was just one element of a naturist subculture which never ceased to amaze our visitors, who were expecting German formality. In the parks, naked men would stroll around grilling sausages on the barbecue. Elsewhere, I have highlighted the paradox of Berlin's free-thinking culture and the city's Prussian heritage of *Ordnung*. This was another such paradox, a fabulous disconnect between extreme informality and the absolute formality of not being allowed to call people by their first names (or what I thought of as 'death by *Sie* form'). I liked to muse on whether the naked men with their barbecue tongs would use the formal *Sie* mode of address when they talked to each other or whether nude conversation slipped more easily into the familiar *Du* form.

As DINKYs (Double Income No Kids Yet) in the reunified city, Liz and I were perfectly placed to enjoy the extensive cultural and social scene in the two Berlins. We, like our friends of the time, have retold these tall, true tales for over 20 years. Life outside the office in Berlin proved unforgettable.

3

THE PROPERTY INDUSTRY: A BLANK PAGE

BERLIN was, quite suddenly, the blank page of the property industry. For the wave of property pioneers, this was both an opportunity and a challenge. The opaque West German real estate market had prime benchmarks and codes of practice – official and unofficial. Berlin, however, had hardly any business community to speak of and no institutional commercial property industry, so we started from scratch. This chapter is about how the profession began to fill that blank page. Mostly, we made it up as we went along.

Prior to 1990, a business community had not really existed in the East because free trade was not permitted to exist, and in the West because the small commercial world was heavily drugged by public subsidies. In the sporting arena, the DDR was infamous for having used artificial means to boost the regime's image in the world. West Berlin had done the same in the business arena. In commercial property, the famous KaDeWe department store may have shone as a symbol of consumer riches in a capitalist oasis, but there had been little open market business prior to *die Wende*. In his famous 'Tear down this Wall!' speech in June 1987, Ronald Reagan taunted Mikhail Gorbachev with an invitation to admire the gleaming shops of the Ku'Damm. Berlin was rarely on any investor's list of cherries to pick out of a portfolio – less than twelve months after Reagan's speech, one of those prime department stores (a Hertie with huge frontage to the Ku'Damm) was dropped from a West German retail property portfolio deal because the investor knew that "Berlin is never going anywhere!" There was a clear discrepancy between Reagan's fine rhetoric and the private sector's perception of how to make money. In the West as in the East, the property page was a blank one at the moment of reunification.

As one of the leaders in the German industry, Weatheralls already had active offices in Frankfurt, Hamburg, Essen, Düsseldorf and Munich, which meant the new Berlin staff were fortunate in having templates for contracts such as leases and mandates. It meant we had German colleagues and German processes where many of our competitors were exporting UK business practices. Interestingly, in addition to the big names such as JLW and Richard Ellis, a cluster of smaller UK agents chose to come and give it a go in Berlin. Drivers Jonas, Vail Williams and Gooch & Wagstaff were established names in the *Estates Gazette* but not in the *Berliner Morgenpost* or *Frankfurter Allgemeine Zeitung*.

Having been mostly trained in valuation and investment work, my personal blank page was learning to be an office agent – and not just an office agent but a *Makler*. The word means 'broker', but to most Germans it carries no connotations of ethics or moral standing. Introducing yourself as an *Immobilienmakler* could lead to short conversations in social situations. As a newly qualified member of the Royal Institution of Chartered Surveyors, I had been trained to manage conflicts of interest. As a *Makler* in Berlin, what was more important was simply managing conflict. Happily, to ease the transition, my company gave me *Makler* training. My coach was the experienced and professional Bernd from our Düsseldorf office, who gave regular guidance on where to plant my feet in a short-termers' market of few ethics.

Bernd flew frequently to Berlin to drill me on the rules of the game, creating formal offer letters with boilerplate text in anticipation of future fee disputes. He also knew how to deal with Berlin's new wave of predatory street lawyers. This legal underworld was working on a blank canvas too, and scavenged in the *Berliner Morgenpost* for ambiguities of property marketing that could earn it a fast buck. The lawyer piranhas would threaten court action before offering to drop the case for a quick cash settlement. Bernd's robust process proved indispensable in that jungle.

One deal example illustrates why we were a clear target for the legal vultures and why, in a dysfunctional market, businesspeople were wary when a *Makler* came calling. In a Ku'damm property we posted fliers advertising a small sublet in the offices of my client, an international property developer. My company was mandated by the lessor but paid by the lessee (a common market practice not just in Berlin but throughout Germany at that time) and did not property manage the building. In essence, we were eating the lunch of the property manager. Today, the *Hausverwaltung* (property management team) would do its job and this fee-earning window would be unlikely to exist. In the dysfunctional market of the time, however, we managed to earn three months' rent from the incoming lessee. The real eye-opener was that the new subtenant we found was located right across the third-floor landing. As the new lessee rang the doorbell for the meeting to sign a contract, their MD ruefully described the red-carpeted landing as "perhaps the most expensive ten metres of my life". Such experiences made businesspeople understandably nervous of the real estate *Makler*.

My own page started to fill up with property market innovations (or at least they were innovations in 1992 in Berlin). A good example was the rent-free period. Berlin headline rents had tripled from DM 30 (per m² per month) to DM 90 in the 24 months since unification. When that euphoria cooled off, softening market sentiment opened the door for rent-free periods to support headline rents, classic cyclical behaviour in the property industry – except that, in Berlin in 1992, no tenant had ever received a *mietfreie Zeit*.

My client, a joint venture of investor Norwich Union and developer Taylor Woodrow, had just weathered a sharp fall in rental values back in the UK where, like everyone else, they had used rent-frees to cushion falling rents. In Berlin, we were the first pioneers to put in place what the clients had just learned in the UK.

Uhlandstraße 14 (U14), the JV's 2,000 m² office development, had initially been marketed for pre-lets at DM 90 per m² per month. When sentiment softened in 1993, asking rents melted like icebergs in the desert. After completion of the U14 building, the unofficial asking rent came down sharply at each monthly letting meeting. The point was that the DM 90 top rent was a mirage, based on a handful of deals in the best buildings. Somewhere around the mid-DM 50 range, we launched the UK-patented stealth weapon: rent-free. We caught the market at a headline rent of DM 50 and signed six lease contracts at that level. In negotiations, I saw how local tenants were wide-eyed at the concept of being allowed to occupy a building without paying rent. When the market later sank below DM 35, that innovation would rapidly look like foresight on the part of the landlord.

Marketing novelties included proper letting brochures, with floor plans to scale and high-quality artists' impressions of the finished product. Just as Berlin had never seen institutional grade buildings, the leasing market had never seen proper brochures. There was also the innovation of the *Musterraum* (show suite) in the many dusty building sites which were fast making new space to let. In the *Musterraum*, tenants could visualise how their furniture would fit in place – a first for Berlin and a competitive advantage in the softening market of the time. Potential tenants were once again astounded at the concept of a furniture salesman drawing sketches of their future office – for free.

Corruption was common in 1990s Berlin and I saw it for myself when the lady owner of one of these furniture businesses offered "a transfer to your Swiss bank account" in return for information on where and when companies were moving. A project manager friend recalls seeing planning officials appear on site to impose mysterious *ad hoc* building stops – which were, in turn, mysteriously cleared if cash payments were made.

"Berlin's developer greyhounds came out of the traps at exactly the same time" – construction in Friedrichstraße 1993 *(photo: Michael Lange)*

The market context of the U14 story is important to recall. Between 1994 and 1996, a decade's worth of Grade A office supply was completed because, as my boss Stuart Reid would say, all the developer greyhounds were coming out of the traps at exactly the same time. Before 1994, office agents like me usually worked with scraps; poor buildings in poor locations such as the 50,000 m² Airport Bureau Center "ABC" near Tegel Airport (a white elephant in an allotment field with no public transport, services or restaurants). Alternatively, we had good buildings in poor locations – over-specified constructions in the back streets of residential neighbourhoods like Steglitz and Lankwitz. At least the latter were small buildings with opportunities for other uses. The ABC elephant would stay largely vacant for a decade.

In 1992 and 1993, U14 was thus a rare thing: a good new building in a good location. The mixed-use U14 was a microcosm of much of the property industry at that time. The rectangular plot of land, in a main side street off the Ku'Damm, comprised a neglected horseshoe shaped residential building to the rear and land with permission to build offices to the front. Post-*Wende*, the site was traded a couple of times (once by Gerald Ronson's Heron Group) before my clients finally built out the *Baulücke* (literally 'building hole'). At the *Grundsteinlegung* (laying of the foundation stone) event to mark the start of construction, the speech by the investor from Norwich highlighted the irony of the British constructing a building to fill a gap in the street which had been created by the Royal Air Force in 1944.

The value of U14 was 90-95% loaded to the new offices at the front, even if the space was equally divided between flats and offices. The low-value ageing residential of U14 was the necessary evil for us to manage and the neglected flats to the rear consumed our time and energy. Today, Berlin residential is one of Europe's strongest growing sectors, but in the 1990s leases were still governed by a legacy of World War II. The 1948 Act was created *in extremis* to give people roofs over their heads by freezing rents during the privations of the infamous Soviet Blockade – when life in Berlin was so extreme that war widows were still carrying away tons of rubble in prams. Residential property law was one page of the property profession which was not to be rewritten in the pioneering post-*Wende* days.

The flats at U14 were in poor condition and were very cheap to occupy. The daily rent was equivalent to five or six euros (for a 60 m² apartment in the city centre of the West), so it was no surprise that the owners did not choose to invest much in the fabric of the property. The same 1948 property law also prevented market uplifts after vacant possession. Despite the prices, the tenants complained a lot (a signature behaviour in Berlin) and the channel for those complaints was the property manager of the joint venture – i.e. me! Most came directed through the tiny and manipulative *Hausmeisterin*, Frau Schrenk. She had been resident at U14 before the Wall went up in 1961. Occasionally, I would be invited behind the net curtains of her ground floor flat to hear the woes of the new Berlin. I would learn whose tap was dripping, whose grouting was flaking away and who was making too much noise after nightfall (usually the foreigners). I would explain that, as she knew, the landlords had no budget for repairing taps and grouting. This energy-sapping process was on-the-job professional development. Poor residential stock was a major feature of the 1990s property industry in Berlin and the clear legacy of the still-open wound of extreme times.

The other big entry in my hypothetical Berlin 'time sheet', was the acquisition of a new 3,000 m² embassy property for the Government of Thailand. The government sector was on every agent's mailshot list, so such business was a common slice of Berlin life. In mid-1991 the German government had narrowly voted to move from Bonn to Berlin, meaning most nations would be upgrading from consulates to embassies. I introduced the Thais to Waterglade, the developer of a prestigious looking scheme (part refurbishment, part new-build) in a leafy street of western Steglitz, a location which scored well on the 'Playground Index', an invention of Stuart Reid, whose five young children had given him a close insight into the unusually high ratio of kids' playgrounds in west Berlin. The *Kinderspielplatzindex* was a tangible measure of the subsidies in west Berlin and became our barometer of gentrification.

The Thai deal took 1,000 days to close and I had regular meetings in the old Thai Consulate in that time. Here, I learned the value of patience when dealing in the codified business culture of Asians. The Thai elder statesman sat reflectively in his impressive throne-like chair, often with eyes closed in meetings. He was a large man with a large presence who looked disconcertingly like the big Buddha in the consulate's entrance hall. Everyone else at the consulate was much smaller and very deferential to the wisdom of the consul. Much polite conversation was exchanged over many cups of tea. Much scepticism came from our Frankfurt head office as to whether the Thais were "for real" in the deal. The head office paranoia was explained by Stuart who had worked in Weatheralls' Tokyo office before running Berlin. He taught me that in business with Asians, what you see and what you hear is not necessarily what you get. The Thais at the consulate were too polite to complain in person, but would follow up a meeting with a two-paragraph fax in heated language which bore no relation to what had just been discussed face to face.

After many months of polite discussion, there came a memorable day when we were instructed to appear at Lepsiusstraße for the inspection of the building site by the Royal Minister for Embassies. This proved to be an enlightening moment in our understanding of our client's hierarchy. When the team from Bangkok got off their smart black bus to inspect the site, they marched slowly in a long single file – keeping a respectful distance from each other and in strict order of seniority. The thirty people (all men) in the hierarchy snake were all wearing black suits, blue ties and crisp white shirts. My friend, the Buddha Consul, was only about number nine in that line. My younger day-to-day contact was so far back that he was lost round the corner in the next cross street.

So much for the international arena. Local human resources in this brave new world were often blunt instruments with neither real estate training nor experience in the business community. The established local agents such as Braun Immobilien (who, coincidentally, wore brown suits) were old-style brokers relying on networks of contacts. However, with business evolving so fast, those old brown-suited networks were of diminishing value. These one-dimensional locals were about 'who you know' not 'what you know'.

Liz's German professional development was more exotic and intrepid than my more international experience. She was a recently qualified UK chartered surveyor employed to value all types of property throughout east Germany for a mortgage lender, the *Bayerische Hypotheken-und-Wechsel Bank (Hypobank)*. The bank was a big Bavarian institution, so before she was allowed to start work in Berlin, Liz was sent to Munich for a month of brainwashing in the bank's procedures and Bavarian company culture. This Munich was not today's Munich, the urbane, globalised and multicultural Exporeal city; the Munich of 1992 was parochial and inward-looking, even in the eyes of other Germans.

In that context, my then-fiancée was also a professional pioneer – a chartered surveyor who was also a foreigner and a young woman added up to something very different for the *Hypobank*. Her working life was a valuable insight on domestic business and how the Germans were filling the 'blank page'. In spite of the bank's human resources adventure with Frau Watson (Liz described herself as their guinea pig), the corporate culture in the Berlin office was firmly old-school. At each end of the working day she punched in and punched out with a time-clock card. In a gap year job in the *Sauerland*, I had once clocked in and out from an industrial production line. It was eye-opening that the same could still apply in the service sector. The blank page of the *Hypobank* was being written in formal Bavarian prose.

Old-style business in West Berlin had floated along on the morphine of government subsidies. Liz's colleague Herr Staub (literally meaning 'dust') was very representative of that comfortable former life. Herr Staub was formal, xenophobic and chauvinistic. He was also close to retirement and grumpy that the office had moved away from his familiar Ernst Reuter Platz in the West to Checkpoint Charlie – or to be more precise, what Herr Staub considered to be just the wrong side of the former checkpoint, in the old East at Friedrichstraße 58-60. His most memorable contribution to my wife's professional development was to teach her how to get in and out of the former DDR as fast as possible. He showed her how to sketch out driving instructions to pin to the steering wheel before venturing into the 'Wild East'. Like many West Berliners, the dusty Herr Staub was fundamentally unhappy that the Wall had disappeared, disturbing his ordered and materially comfortable life.

In the old DDR, the blankest page of Liz's professional life as a property valuer was a total absence of comparable transactions. Her patch was to the east of Berlin close to the border with Poland – towns such as Cottbus and Frankfurt an der Oder where there were, naturally, no open-market transactions comparable for valuation purposes. This meant her valuation team had to make things up as they went along, which started by quizzing the planning authorities on infrastructure projects in the pipeline and applying old-fashioned gut feeling about the future.

Happily, as well as the old guard of Herr Staubs, the *Hypobank* was also staffed by open minds who thrived on the opportunities of Berlin's blank page. In former DDR days, Liz's East German colleague Barbara Freiberger had specialised in public relations for the state owned business of frozen storage in fish trawlers. Hers was the real professional blank canvas. She started as a secretary at the bank and worked her way up. If trained property professionals from the UK or West Germany were having to start from scratch in new territories, then imagine how clean Barbara's blank page was. No training, no market, no comparables. 25 years later, the *Hypobank* has been the *Hypovereinsbank* since the 1998 merger and Frau Freiberger has lived a successful professional life and raised young German children with wide horizons.

The blank page of the Berlin property industry has long since been inked in. The internationals have mainly come and gone and it is Germans who are designing the future. A generation later, every other citizen of Berlin is a *Zugezogene* – an incomer from outside the city – who consider themselves to be Germans rather than 'East' Berliners or 'West' Berliners. Herr Staub is long since retired and it is the open-minded Barbara Freibergers who are writing the much-in-demand book of Berlin's future.

Frau Watson's property valuation challenge *(photo: Gerd Danigel)*

4   PIONEERS AND THICK CIGARS

EXTRAORDINARY times attract extraordinary people. During my thousand days in the city, Berlin was the hub of the development business and a magnet for the cream of the world's property developers. Some were my clients. For me, having sidestepped the established London corporate hierarchy by speaking fluent German, I got direct access to these fascinating entrepreneurs while still a very young property professional.

Berlin's fearless developer pioneers had abundant energy and a willingness to gamble. Since the global financial crisis, many 'value add' or 'opportunistic' property funds have taken up some of the ground these individuals previously occupied. Back then, however, these men were still real developers – taking personal liabilities and betting their own money, plus as much bank finance as they could borrow. In 1995, the development industry was rocked by the antics of Germany's leading private developer, Dr Jürgen

Schneider, who had successfully hoodwinked the main German lending banks for years. When the big banks carried out valuations of his properties, Dr Schneider conjured up non-existent lease contracts, thousands of extra square metres and even a few imaginary floors on the roofs of his buildings. The illusionist was the Severus Snape of German real estate. He eventually had to flee Germany, but when he was tracked down in Miami, the huge scale of the fraud emerged and he was imprisoned. The developer pioneers I knew in Berlin were still operating (just) in the pre-Schneider era – before tighter controls and falling values restricted the oxygen of debt finance.

In his obituary in both *The Times* and *The Daily Telegraph*, Ronald 'Ronnie' Lyon was described as "larger than life". *The Times* recalled him as a "fat cat with many lives", a reference to his corporate bankruptcies and reinventions, though he never seemed to incur personal bankruptcy. Ronnie was not afraid of exploring new territories and foreign cultures. In 1972, just before the UK joined the European Economic Community, he boldly set up Lyon Holdings in Paris. It was liquidated in 1974. Extravagant Ronnie would yo-yo between boom and bust and was renowned in the UK as 'the inventor of the industrial estate'. He was known to be generous with money – especially when it came from a bank – and famously never allowed anyone else to pay a restaurant or bar bill.

Ronnie Lyon

When I got to know him in Berlin, Ronnie was in his mid-sixties, short and overweight. His pale skin had the unhealthy sheen of a driven workaholic. That was no coincidence: Ronnie loved to cram sixty minutes into every hour and lots of waking hours into a day – the hallmark of the entrepreneurial and very successful.

Before starting his working day in the office, Ronnie used the early hours to get ahead of the competition. For him, this meant driving out into the countryside to view property. For me, it meant getting out of bed before 5am to pick him up before 6am and drive around the Berliner Ring orbital.

I thought of it as a Dawn Drive on a safari. After a couple of hours looking at development sites off cobbled roads in old East Germany, I would return Ronnie to the Grand Hotel in the city centre so that he could put in another 15 hours with bankers, planners, mayors, agents, occupiers and lawyers. Ronnie Lyon had an insatiable appetite for business.

By turns, Ronnie would be charming and offensive – "Hello, Dr Watson, are we doing house calls today?" – followed by – "You're just a glorified taxi driver!" – which he shot out drily without a hint of irony. There was no way of telling which Ronnie Lyon I would pick up at dawn.

One sunny spring morning, Ronnie asked to stop for breakfast in rural Brandenburg. If the city centre of east Berlin was a culinary black hole, it was almost impossible to find anything that would satisfy Ronnie in the fields of the former DDR. Especially not at 9am. By great good fortune, I found a *Gasthaus* and got the owner out of bed. Keen to impress my famous client, I persuaded the proprietor to rustle up Ronnie's request of fried eggs and bacon. Both the farm eggs and the *Speck* – the nearest German equivalent to British bacon – were certainly fresh. I knew that because the owner had to walk over a field to get them from his friend, the pig farmer. Napkin over his chalk-stripe suit, Ronnie mopped up the egg yolk and volunteered that eating bacon and eggs in the sun was one of the happiest things in life. He was so satisfied, in fact, that he insisted on paying – and here the morning idyll ended and the trouble began. Ronnie was famously generous with money, but this particular offer was not about generosity.

In front of our disbelieving host, Ronnie produced a thickly padded roll of notes from the top pocket of his RL-monogrammed shirt. The only visible note was a DM 500 (€260) – considerably more money than many citizens had earned in a month in the DDR – and Ronnie slowly and purposefully put the crisp 500 note on the table. Repeatedly and stubbornly, he shrugged off my pleas to put a few coins down for the DM 4.75 bill. Ronnie's anti-German streak, formed during the war, was never far from the surface and from the look on his face, I realised he was enjoying goading the locals and this was not really about the bill. I found the words to translate Ronnie's expression,

39

"tell him I have nothing smaller", and as both a German speaker and Germanophile, I willed the ground to swallow me up.

Our host knocked on doors around the little rural village and eventually rounded up the change he needed. Goodness knows what he told his neighbours about the two capitalists in ties and pinstripe suits. Finally, the owner returned with 25 pfennigs and 495 Deutschmarks. Ronnie lit up a thick cigar and carefully left the 25 pfennigs as a breakfast tip. He would not allow me to add to that.

Ronnie always stayed in east Berlin's Grand Hotel, the best in the East, although that was not saying so much. As the top hotel in the Russian sector, the Grand attracted a lot of international guests, and for that reason it was known to have been a magnet for spies and riddled with listening devices. In my time in Berlin, it still felt like a place where John le Carré characters would pop up in the vast lobby, smoking high-tar cigarettes. The Grand was also the unofficial HQ for Berlin's new real estate pioneers. One evening, I waited in the huge lobby for Ronnie to arrive from the airport. He was late and it was before the age of mobile phones. As ever in those days, we just waited patiently. For once, instead of Tegel, Ronnie had flown in to Schönefeld, east Berlin's old-style airport. In 1993 it had only a single luggage carousel for bags which still mostly came from destinations such as Havana, Bucharest and Kiev.

Ronnie's RL-monogrammed leather bag had been mislaid by the baggage handlers, which meant that RL watched that single carousel turn. And turn and turn. Eventually the bag was found and he arrived at the Grand in a rage, spluttering invective about Bomber Harris and The Germans. At the front desk, a purple-faced Ronnie slammed his briefcase on the counter and vented, loudly, to the polite concierge as well as most of the curious lobby: "Your airport is hopeless! If I had wanted to go to the Third World, I would have flown to fucking Ethiopia!"

Ronnie's joint venture, Nobleclear, was one of a number of entrepreneurial vehicles set up by Godfrey Bradman, another of Berlin's big developer characters. Bradman, sometimes nicknamed God, had made a fortune with Broadgate in London. An Orthodox Jew, he was famously picky about food (lots of allergies) drink (no alcohol) and smoking (would not tolerate any passive smoking). Ronnie, by contrast, had no food allergies, drank lots of alcohol and was never far from a big cigar. In restaurants, Godfrey would ask, anxiously, about where and how glasses had been washed. Ronnie would just ask for another glass. When the two partners were in the same room it made for a people-watching gala – especially over a lunch or dinner.

Howard Ronson had made a fortune developing office buildings in New York and, like Ronnie, had experience in Paris. He swiftly explored and rejected commercial property in Berlin, correctly judging that there would be no demand for offices until the infrastructure was in place a generation later.

Like Ronnie, Howard concentrated for a time on developing plots of residential. Also like Ronnie, he was never far from a cigar. One evening in our Unter den Linden office, I ran development appraisals while the big bosses settled in the meeting room to smoke cigars and chew the fat with Howard. As Weatheralls Germany did not yet have a mouse, we navigated basic Excel spreadsheets with cursors. In

Howard Ronson

the pre-mouse era, working through a spreadsheet cell by cell was like moving a rook around a chessboard: there were no diagonal moves.

Three times, I entered the *fumatoria* of a meeting room to get instructions to play with more numbers. On the fourth occasion, Howard Ronson pointed to the new sensitivity analyses, narrowed his eyes and said to me:

"Do you know what you are doing?"

"No, Mr Ronson, what is that?"

"Intellectual masturbation, that's what…"

Whatever the interpretation, Howard did not build out in Berlin in the early 1990s and that proved a shrewd decision. A few years later, his timing was equally shrewd in Paris and he made a lot of money there building out at the right time.

These giant characters captured the attention of one of the great personalities of the UK press.Our press trip in Berlin in late 1992 was a Big Night Out in a city where nearly every night out was immense. Chris Warman, *The Times*'s influential property correspondent came along too but the star turn was Bruce Kinloch, *The Daily Telegraph*'s property correspondent and long-lunch legend.

Kinloch's *nom de plume* was "Rory Ferguson" (his children were called Rory and Fergus), and in the UK, that column was reckoned to be the most interesting and insightful property read of its day. Bruce was described by *The Spectator* as the "worst behaved man of his time" and much of his Rory Ferguson material was sourced at huge-drinking lunches and dinners. Like Ronnie and Howard, Bruce loved to smoke big cigars and was afraid of nothing.

Stuart Reid knew the Kinloch drill, having once taken Bruce out on a huge bender in Tokyo. The Reid business mantra, refined by nights out after work in the Far East, was "never go to bed before the client". Stuart rigidly

Weatherall Green & Smith Press Outing in Berlin 1992
Left to Right: Stuart Reid (WGS), Chris Warman (The Times), Chris Bull-Diamond (WGS), Brian Mitchell (Mitchell Purvis), Andy Watson (WGS), Bruce Kinloch (The Daily Telegraph) – with cigar in hand!

practised what he preached too, and in Berlin that required stamina. Chris Bull-Diamond came along to ensure Bruce had a memorable time. When he arrived in reception, Chris had each of us tell ten friends to call the office at five-minute intervals. He wanted the press to feel the energy of a bustling place and for an hour, our office reception hummed with noise like a trading floor.

We warmed up in a typically dark bar in east Berlin. After three Warsteiner beers, the *Daily Telegraph* correspondent started launching cardboard beer mats across the room like frisbees. After three more beers, he was aiming (accurately) at the local east Germans, who responded in kind. The place kicked off. Bruce had built his reputation on getting out and about. He did not disappoint as we finished after four in the morning. On a Thursday.

Chris Bull-Diamond himself loved a big cigar and was certainly a pioneer – of the previous generation. As a young man still in his twenties and despite speaking little German, he opened the Weatherall Green and Smith business in Frankfurt in 1973. He succeeded by being a strong communicator and a shrewd, charismatic businessman with high energy and a fine sense of timing. He built a network of offices across Germany but had never dreamed Weatheralls would one day open in Berlin. Before *die Wende*, Chris had run Germany for 16 years but visited what he called the "backwater" of Berlin just twice – and one of those was when Lufthansa was forced to divert his flight from Hamburg.

"CBD" had a lively sense of humour about all things – except money. Fees were not amusing. Chris' management style was switching frequently between stick and carrot. By turns, his staff would get clipped round the ear and then encouraged with an amusing anecdote or a peculiar nickname. Tall and imposing, Chris was an old-fashioned boss who brought out decanters of whisky in his vast personal office at five o'clock. His legendary client event on a boat at Henley was hard-drinking corporate entertaining from before the era of ethics officers. As the sun set at the end of a long hot summer's day, I recall two of Chris's most senior partners took out a nine iron and started lofting golf balls from off the deck towards some distant greenhouses on the far side of the river Thames. In the company Bentley on the way home, a well-lubricated and unusually satisfied Chris offered me the advice that keeping clients happy was more important than writing reports or compiling spreadsheets: "What counts are clients. Just get this client stuff right and the rest takes care of itself". His clients respected him and his staff were inspired by him. Chris Bull-Diamond's recent passing last autumn marks the end of the era of the first generation of pioneers in Germany. The property industry is a smaller place without him.

The big Berlin characters in my life were not just cigar-smoking Brits. I came into regular contact with German investors like the debonair Busso von Alvensleben of Hammerson and the smooth Swede, Kennet Carlsson. As it happened, both of them were fond of a cigar too. Carlsson was a successful tech entrepreneur, one of a group of Swedish private individuals who singed their fingers when tax breaks lured them into European property investment in the early 1990s. In Berlin, he had developed a very over-specified construction in a backstreet location of a minor suburb. With each lease we slowly signed up, an appreciative Kennet bought me several Sambucas – his "favourite drink for making daughters" (of which he had four already).

The memorable characters of Berlin also included local German colleagues – from both West and East. They were not developers or huge real estate names like Ronnie Lyon and Howard Ronson but they were definitely pioneers in the sense that, unlike the internationals, this was their first real estate experience.

Klaus 'Alan' Heck was a salesman from western Germany who came to make his fortune in the El Dorado of Berlin. Tall, blond, good looking and 40ish, he might have had experience of selling car radios or air conditioning but certainly not commercial property. He adapted swiftly to flogging plots of serviced industrial land and in doing so confirmed to me that years of training to be a chartered surveyor were not very useful for being a successful real estate *Makler*. In the tough world of the *Makler*, Klaus was a *Makler's Makler*, with skin as thick as a Panzer tank.

The Panzer was, however, just one aspect of his persona, as Herr Heck had led an intriguing double life. In a previous existence selling things in

England, he had polished an unusually upper-class way of speaking the Queen's English and was so taken with his cultured 'Anglo persona' that he gave himself a new name – 'Alan'. This was no dormant middle name – he actively answered to Alan for his international contacts. The two Hecks, Klaus and Alan, were an absorbing Dr Jekyll and Mr Hyde: blunt-instrument German *Makler* on the one hand, silver-tongued English gent on the other.

On the phone, Klaus/Alan used a headset with an earpiece, which gave him the look of a salesman at the drive-thru counter of a Burger King. He said it allowed him to be more focused on selling while speaking. In action, he would close his eyes and launch into cold-call overdrive for the latest victim from the phone book. In our open office space there were four agents, and Herr Heck made more noise than the other three put together. His name was an onomatopoeia: a word which phonetically imitates the source of the sound. I came to think of hecking as a verb. When he spoke, Klaus Heck clicked his consonants. Klaus hecked: "*Heck. Heck. Heck. Heck. Heck.*"

My East German colleague Marc was a whispering anti-Heck. He was one of the rare Easterners to have worked abroad – in the DDR's New York embassy in the mid-1980s. He told a delightful story of having successfully persuaded the East German government to keep up with the tech-savvy capitalists and invest in a new state-of-the-art device at the embassy. It was a fax machine. Marc's new toy, however, sat mostly silent, because few of the other Communist regimes owned a fax machine and none of the western governments communicated freely with the DDR.

Marc was in his early forties, but the day-to-day moral choices of diplomatic service in East Germany's system had put a lot of miles on his clock. Having a passport in the DDR came at a price. Marc sat opposite me in the office and would usually arrive in the mornings with streaming eyes and bad breath. He reeked sweetly of spirits and stale tobacco through the Fisherman's Friends which he crunched to mask the odour. Marc chain-smoked Marlboro Red cigarettes with trembling fingers. His quivering hand could not grip the pen, making his handwriting spidery and nearly illegible. Beneath the scars of history was an intelligent man who had lost his way in the moral pollution of the DDR. Behind the watering eyes were untold stories – or at least untold to his western colleagues.

Like many former DDR citizens, Marc reinvented himself as a real estate professional, as property broking required no particular license or training in Germany. Marc certainly knew people and sometimes surprisingly well – if they were from the East. He spoke German with the lilting sing-song accent of Saxony with long and sweeping vowel sounds. I realised how he had been keeping his German simple for my benefit when he spoke to fellow Saxons on the phone. When he slipped into his distinct dialect it sounded to me as if he had switched on a scrambler device. Professionally, Marc's big achievement was carefully assembling a residential development site for Ronnie Lyon in a rural village to the south of Berlin, federating the interests of over 40 separate owners of agricultural land plots. Like watching Ronnie and Godfrey, seeing Ronnie and Marc working together was pure gold for people watchers. Between Ronnie's thick cigars and Marc's Marlboros, they would smoke up a storm. Ronnie recognised that Marc's unique ability to persuade east German farmers to sell land was key to his prospects for making money, so he resisted his natural inclination to put him down and would plead in his most charming voice: "Marc, can you *please* speak to the people in Blankenfelde?"

Then there were The Russians. The Russian underworld loved Berlin not just because it was the easternmost city with a western-quality lifestyle, but also because there were still almost 400,000 Russian citizens living in the old East German barracks. When Moscow played Berlin at football, these same Russians warmed up with vodka, drove to the match in a convoy of armoured cars and filled the Olympic Stadium. From mid-1994, the Soviet military took their marching orders and returned to the bankrupt Motherland, having sold their weapons, hats, badges and just about anything that could not be bolted down. This was fertile recruitment ground for the underworld and some Russian military people, like the East Germans, stayed and reinvented themselves as capitalists.

In 1993, I leased a small suite of offices to a Russian import-export company which satisfied the institutional owner's requirements of a six-month bank guarantee and paying a market rent. These days, requirements to Know Your Client (KYC), would probably not have let that transaction through the legal and compliance net. Before signing their lease, the Russians asked me to go to a Kempinski Hotel room to settle my company's letting fee (as explained earlier, the local market practice was to be retained by the landlord but take a fee from the tenant). As if in a movie, they opened a black bag containing the exact amount – over DM 38,000 (€20,000). I was taken aback and asked for a bank transfer. At that point, I was not the only one to be wrong-footed – the new tenants were baffled that anyone would be so peculiar as to refuse cash.

To celebrate their new premises (which I would later see furnished with a huge leather sofa, giant TV screen and some games consoles), the importers and exporters invited me and my wife to dine at the famous Kempinski Hotel. The night was memorable for the savage Berlin winter weather, but the Russians came dressed in fur hats and thick boots and looked very at home in the deep November snow.

Their team was diverse: the smooth greying boss Viktor, who looked like Richard Gere, his stunning 19-year-old girlfriend with huge black eyes and white porcelain skin, the sweaty Joker who could not stop recounting stories, the silent Heavy who always had his hand in the pocket of his thick great coat. Then there was the Fixer, a taxi driver from west Berlin who doubled as their chauffeur and whose value to Viktor was presumably his German passport. After dinner we walked to the Kempinski lounge for the inevitable big cigar. Behind the counter, Richard Gere had a personal bottle of the most expensive cognac inscribed with his name. When The Joker appeared in the lounge, the hotel's grand piano player respectfully stopped playing, silently got up to allow the Russian to take his place at the keys, where he entertained us brilliantly for 30 minutes while the lounge filled up with expensive cigar smoke. Playing the piano was the only thing all night that stopped the Joker telling stories.

Six months later, there was an organised break-in at the office building now occupied by the Russians. As property manager and leasing agent, I had to sacrifice my Sunday morning to visit all the irate tenants. I was not too pleased either. I had worked my way down to the second floor import-export company where I rang and waited at the opaque glass door (a special fit-out installed by the Russians). The door swung slowly open and the Joker-pianist aimed a small gun at my head: "Ah, Mr Watson," he said, putting the revolver away, "you can't be too careful round here." As with the bag of cash, I was taken aback. It all happened so fast that I almost missed it.

Today, the Russian underworld is still present in Berlin but the property world has become much more institutionally acceptable. The cigar-smoking habit has long gone, as have Ronnie, Bruce, Marc, Howard, and now Chris Bull-Diamond. My thousand days in Berlin will always remain memorable for the chance I had to rub shoulders with those exceptional people.

Part Two

OUT OF BERLIN

5 GERMANY'S WILD EAST – OUT OF THE OASIS OF BERLIN

IF the backdrop to life in Berlin was the heavy hand of history, outside the city it was the iron legacy of Communism. My comfortable west Berlin home was an island for exploring the former *Deutsche Demokratische Republik* (DDR) which became known after unification as the *neue Bundesländer* ("new federal states"). Culturally and professionally, Berlin felt like an oasis within the desert of those five states. To me, they usually felt like amplified versions of the many curiosities of urban east Berlin.

For the post-*Wende* generation, there were not many success stories in the bleak economic landscape outside Berlin – but I ended up having a hand in a big one. Coca-Cola's development in the former DDR has become emblematic of the *Zeitgeist* of the early 1990s and the rehabilitation of East Germany. As the reader will see in the following chapters, I played a very small role in that success. It started with a routine cold call and ended with the company building a 160,000 m² plant producing over 50 million bottles a year. The social, economic and political background to that story begins in this chapter, which is about my memorable experiences in the new states, a long way from the twin hearts of urban Berlin.

It is worth recalling the political and social context of the former DDR. Right up until it happened, *die Wende* was unthinkable. In June 1989, one of the essay questions for my university finals was the old chestnut *Deutsche Wiedervereinigung: Traum oder Realität?* – German Reunification: Dream or Reality? It popped up every three years and I felt comfortable that I had prepared the right material for a well-reasoned essay on this standard subject. Like all young people conditioned by the Cold War, I answered 'Dream'. Twenty weeks later, the Wall came down.

The economic context was that if the underinvested capital of the DDR was wholly unprepared to cope with that surprising turn of events, then that was doubly true of the five new states. In *Hauptstadt* Berlin (the Eastern part), environmental pollution was at shocking levels and roads were very neglected. Both these heavy legacies were amplified in the *neue Bundesländer* (NBL).

Just getting out of Berlin by car was often an adventure in itself. The legacy of little infrastructure investment for 50 years was a terrible road network with surfaces which were poor, very poor or just plain dangerous. Motorway slip roads were small and blind with incredibly tight angles. Sometimes there were no entrance or exit lanes at all and goods traffic lumbered on and off fast roads at right angles. Dual carriageways were sometimes surfaced with cobblestones and would become very slippery when wet – even with the good grip of west German tyres.

The contrast between East and West was at its most extreme on the roads, and the sense of peril was only heightened by the two-speed nature of the traffic. Quite literally: on the one hand, there were the cars of the East, the Wartburgs, Skodas and the signature car of the DDR, the two-stroke Trabant, with 26 horsepower and a top speed of 100 km/h (downhill with a following wind). It was said that in former times, the DDR speed limit had been set at 100 km/h because, even disregarding the crumbling roads, only cars from the

51

West could physically move faster than that. Stopping a Western driver to hand out a speeding ticket was, of course, like successful big game hunting for an official in the DDR.

On the other hand, there were the powerful Mercedes, BMW, Audis and Porsches of the *Bundesrepublik*. Germans like to drive fast – and this had striking consequences on two-lane motorways that had suddenly been stripped of their speed limits. There was either fast or slow, with nothing in between. In the slow lane were articulated lorries and Trabants all trundling along at the speed of the slowest. In the fast lane was the rest, flying past. Nipping from the slow lane to the fast lane required a steely nerve, a long careful check of the rear view mirror, swift reactions and rapid acceleration. Joining the *Autobahn* from a blind slip road often necessitated a quick prayer.

Judging from the many broken vehicles abandoned by the roadside, the thin plastic bodywork of a Trabant did not hold up well in an accident. In fact, Liz and I witnessed a frightening pile-up on a narrow and busy motorway in a forest near Potsdam. A big lorry on the opposite carriageway misjudged the move into the fast lane, clipped another truck and thundered diagonally through the central reservation, splintering the metal barrier like plywood before flipping over on its side. Now directly in our path, the horizontal vehicle slid towards us as if in slow motion. It stopped moving about eight car lengths in front of our little Honda Civic. Silence followed. I can still feel my heart beat faster as I write this. That accident left quite an impression on me and heightened the sense of excitement on the roads of the former DDR.

The challenges of getting from A to B were complicated further by the big navigational hurdles of that time: poor maps and renamed streets. Throughout 1991, many streets in the East had been rebranded, usually by replacing communist icons with bland generic names (Karl-Marx-Park, for example, would become Stadtpark). The already hopeless and outdated maps of the NBL just could not keep up with the pace of change. Sometimes, the names on the map were correct but the tarmac just petered out. More commonly, roads were interrupted by massive and uncharted roadworks laying drains or phone lines – which meant turning the car around for a long diversion. In the era before SMS, email, mobile phone or GPS, it was always necessary to leave extra time to get lost before a meeting. In the early 1990s East, there were also no public phone boxes. 'Never Lost' did not exist.

If not exactly inviting, the former DDR did guarantee memorable leisure excursions. The five NBL were certainly cheap. Excursions had a real fairytale quality and included Potsdam's yellow palace, the Harz mountains of the Brothers Grimm and the pretty hills and woods of *Sächsische Schweiz* (Saxon Switzerland) not far from Dresden.

die Spreewald – river Spree and Kraftwerk Vetschau in the 1980s

One of the strangest excursions was the Spreewald, to the south of Berlin. In the relative context of the DDR, the Spreewald was regarded as a jewel of nature. With its flat-bottomed boats, green meadows and tree-lined canals, the area was similar to the Norfolk Broads or France's Marais Poitevin (*'la Venise Verte'*). Similar, with one glaring difference – in 1993, the Spreewald shared those canals with the huge Vetschau power station. Gondoliers in the Venice of East Germany punted tourists past giant smokestacks belching fumes with the oddly sweet odour of brown coal.

Smokestacks and gondoliers were just one sharp contrast which exemplified the bizarre urban planning of the DDR – and that, remember, was considered one of the country's finest leisure experiences. In the name of Five Year Plans and industry, the built environment had been consistently degraded and abused in the NBL. In the early 1990s, town centres, especially in the south, were dark from industrial pollution. Jet-black Halle was the most striking example I saw. Environmental *Altlasten* (literally "old burdens") surfaced all the time, reflecting the DDR's reckless disregard for the environment. Contamination was everywhere. Raw sewage, for example, was systematically dumped into *Rieselfelder* (sewage fields) without a thought for tomorrow. Then there were the 400,000 soldiers of the Soviet Army who still occupied no less than 400,000 square miles of the DDR. The conquering Russians (as they saw it) cared even less than the DDR regime about pollution and the effects on Germany's long-term physical environment. When, at the settling of the Two Plus Four Treaty in September 1990, the time came to negotiate payment for the clean-up of their 45 years of pollution, the bankrupt Soviets just washed their hands completely and pointed out who had started the Great Patriotic War in the first place.

Beyond the legacies of poor roads and pollution, travelling into 'real' east Germany provided me with some vivid memories, starting with McDonald's, one of the favourite destinations for Easterners crossing to the West to explore for the first time. The new citizens of the *Bundesrepublik* initially engaged in an orgy of retail spending on what were seen as Western trophies – jeans, junk food and pornography. Across the NBL, planning permissions and restrictive opening hours were ignored by the authorities for a time and tents were allowed to spring up selling all sorts of stuff to satisfy the thirst for spending money.

In 1992, I travelled by train to look at Leipzig's high street retail and improvise a handwritten traders' plan of the main streets and the famous covered galleries of the Altstadt. I had logged a small McDonald's at the Hauptbahnhof and was saving this treat (and at the time it genuinely was worth a detour in the former DDR) for the end of my day. I thought I had left myself enough time to grab a takeaway for the train home and was happy to see only two families ahead of me at the single open till. Even if I never got my Fisch Mac and Cola Light, what happened next has remained engraved in my memory for life.

The people in front of me were discovering how McDonald's worked. Item by item, these 'first-time buyers' went through the menu on the wall which I (like most kids from the West) had known by heart since the age of ten. For each product, the conversation went along these lines:

"What, exactly, is in a Big Mac?"

"Two all-beef patties, special sauce, melted cheese etc."

"OK, but what if we don't want your special sauce?"

"Then you would need to wait a while whilst we make another hamburger for you."

"OK, but surely the Big Mac is cheaper without the sauce?"

"No. It's always the same price."

"That's strange. What price is it if you take out the gherkins?"

"The same price."

"I prefer my gherkins from the Spreewald. Where are yours from?"

And so on and so on. I forgot about the train and enjoyed the child-like enjoyment of seeing the stale routines of the Western world being reinvented.

The former DDR felt even more curious outside the major cities. If Leipzig was a big city with clear real estate potential, Wittenberge in deepest east Germany most definitely was not. In Wittenberge, I had a memorable instruction to advise Ronnie Lyon in working through a planning gain situation. The planning authorities of the State of Brandenburg understood enough about capitalism to offer a trade-off, where in return for granting planning permission for a prime 150-hectare site near the Berliner Ring, they required a *quid pro quo* from Ronnie to develop an industrial estate outside Wittenberge. Ronnie was fine with that principle – so long as he never had to waste his valuable time on a three-hour round trip to Wittenberge. This is how, in the name of keeping our client happy, I ended up driving that round trip several times.

The town was a microcosm of what was happening across the NBL. Wittenberge, with a population of about 40,000, lies on the river Elbe, halfway between Berlin and Hamburg. On paper, not so disastrous. The big problem was the mono-industrial policy of the DDR, which had determined that the town's chosen industry in the town would be sewing machines. And very little else. When the Wall came down, the old-style Veritas sewing machines of the East were, of course, uncompetitive both to produce and to service with spare parts.

Ghost Town on the Elbe – Empty Wittenberge in the 1990s

The *Treuhandanstalt* (THA) was the organisation responsible for liquidating state-owned businesses in former East Germany and was faced with a massive and thankless task. At one point, the THA were guardians of a land bank the size of the state of Saxony-Anhalt. In Wittenberge, the THA took the tough decision to shut the big Veritas factory and the economy of the town came to a sudden and violent halt. Overnight, unemployment rose to over 50% – in the context of a Communist regime which had previously engineered 100% employment. Elsewhere, all over the East, the same was happening. The net result was that talented people moved to the West, with its hope and its opportunities. Many from Wittenberge swiftly found they missed the comfort of social cohesion and regretted the new capitalist freedom thing.

When I first drove there in my Honda Civic, Wittenberge was like a ghost town. In April 1945 the town had been bombarded and then largely destroyed in a pincer movement of the Russians and the Americans, shortly before the meeting of the armies of the superpowers on the Elbe. Because of the DDR's emphasis on building apartment blocks outside the town centre, the historic Altstadt had never been rebuilt since 1945 and was mostly empty and crumbling. The *Rathaus* (town hall) was blackened by pollution and looked like a prison.

As previously seen in the context of the Spreewald, centralist urban planning in the DDR had been, to say the least, inconsistent. My first meeting in Wittenberge's *Rathaus* with the new urban planning team (comprising most of the same personnel as the old planning team) was also a thoroughly odd moment. Keen to make a good impression in my best chalk-stripe suit and yellow silk tie, I sat opposite a suspicious and unwelcoming planning official in open-toed sandals, beige socks and a well-worn cardigan. Trying not to be patronising, I explained what we were intending to do to regenerate his town. I stuck to the script, which was that Mr Lyon had no intention of investing there unless there was a pre-let or firm commitment from an occupier. In five minutes, I had already seen enough of Wittenberge to know that barring a miracle, there would not be a pre-let. It was, in its own way, a bit of a Leipzig McDonald's moment. Going through the steps of the property development process with the sandal-wearing local official felt like explaining the contents of a Big Mac to a first-time buyer.

When I used the word "speculative", (in the context of building an industrial development which was not secured with a pre-lease) the flashpoint between the perspectives of Communism and Capitalism was reached. It may have been the fault of my German language skills, but the wary official clearly understood "speculation" – in the sense of making huge profits. He abruptly stood up and walked out – shouting that he would "not allow a foreigner, and, worse, a young foreigner, to kick sand in his face."

This had not been a good start. I got a better reception over lunch with the conservative CDU mayor (who was happily a big supporter of the whole planning gain idea). The mayor was worried by the sand-in-the-face speech I had just received. As we drove back to the Altstadt in his comfortable (chauffeured) Volvo, we saw my second-hand Honda, the smartest and most powerful car (with almost 80 horsepower) parked in the street. It was surrounded by at least a dozen men staring at my grey vehicle as if it were a Bentley or Lamborghini. As we got closer, I saw that the F-registered (denoting western Frankfurt am Main) numberplate had been attracting interest from the local police – and had gathered no less than three separate parking tickets in as many hours. The progressive mayor got out and stuffed the tickets awkwardly in his pocket, promising he would "take care of that".

On my next visit to Wittenberge, the cardigan wearer had clearly been gagged. His body language, however, betrayed a barely concealed hostility. Ronnie's mega development on the Berliner Ring never happened as planned and nor, of course, did the little industrial estate in Wittenberge.

Sadly, the town's population has halved since then and more people continue to leak away each year. Most of the young and dynamic citizens of Wittenberge have long gone (many to Berlin), leaving the unemployed and the retired as the heart of today's shrinking community.

In Berlin, urbanisation has reversed the leakage of the brain drain – which was precisely what the Wall had been built to prevent. Since 2007, the German capital has experienced a grassroots recovery and a growing population. That very same global trend has, however, sucked the remaining life out of towns like Wittenberge across the former DDR.

At reunification in 1990, the population of the DDR was over sixteen million. In 2017, there are three million fewer. In that time, Wittenberge, a microcosm of the *neue Bundesländer*, has gone from being a little town of 40,000 to a shrinking village of 18,000. The *Deutsche Demokratische Republik* had given its socialist citizens full employment and a Wall to keep them from moving. Both have long since disappeared.

6 THE BERLINER RING

MY thousand days in Berlin were spent primarily in Berlin. The urban fabric of the two Berlins was where we lived our lives – in and out of the office, with occasional excursions through the former DDR to places such as Wittenberge and Leipzig.

Weatheralls' strategy, however, swiftly evolved to target property outside Berlin's two urban centres. It felt right for our clients to prioritise working with lower-value businesses who were rebuilding east Germany through activities such as resurfacing roads, manufacturing pipes and laying telephone wires.

Our business strategy was, ultimately, more short-term pragmatism than top-down vision. The thinking was twofold: a) the investment market in the urban centres was not ripe for transacting high-margin existing investments and b) industrial land deals out of the city were relatively simple and effective business. Industrial property also levered up our huge out-of-

The Berliner Ring

"For a motorway, it felt oddly serene." The Berliner Ring in 1985 *(photo: Gerd Danigel)*

town instruction at Brandenburg Park and the major land deal we did with Coca-Cola. The following chapters will examine how those two compelling subjects played out. This section is about the Berliner Ring and the genesis of Berlin's new *Gewerbeparks* (business parks).

The Ring round Berlin had a colourful history. Like many of Germany's motorways, the road encircling the city was first built in the 1930s. After the 1945 division of Germany into four zones, the (almost) orbital road fell entirely under Soviet control – meaning that when Germany was reunified 45 years later, much of the dual carriageway had been untouched since the war. Most of the Ring in 1990 looked very similar to the grainy sepia films of the road Hitler constructed.

The experience of driving on the Ring was completely different from the heavy congestion of London's M25. Though the M25 is slightly smaller than the Ring's 200km circumference, there were several times more vehicles in the orbital around London. Since the Ring was some physical distance from both East Berlin and the island of West Berlin, there was, in those immediate post-*Wende* days, simply not much traffic. The uneven surface of the Ring's dual carriageway was in poor order but it remained a pleasant and empty drive bordered by attractive pine forests. For a motorway, it felt oddly serene. In 1992, the Ring still had little of the commercial roadside detritus of the West, with few petrol filling stations, advertising hoardings or fast food outlets. I imagined the Golden Age of driving in the 1950s must have felt like this.

The heaviest traffic was to the south, between the two major junctions to the other big cities of the East, Leipzig to the southwest and Dresden to the southeast. Some stretches of the busier southern Ring even had three lanes, very rare in the former DDR where over 98% of motorways were dual carriageways, unchanged since the 1930s. In 1992, government statistics recorded some 1,300km of six-lane (or even eight-lane) motorways in west Germany. The whole of east Germany had only 40km of *Autobahn* with six lanes.

Outside Berlin, the major hubs were Potsdam and Schönefeld. Historic Potsdam was to the southwest (at eight o'clock on an imaginary clock face) and Schönefeld Airport to the southeast (at five o'clock). Most of the clock face to the north and east attracted nothing more than occasional construction by owner-occupiers. The magnet for business was the 50 km to the south and west of what, since reunification, had been renamed the A10 Berliner Ring.

Potsdam was the (neglected) Versailles of Berlin and looked and felt like it had been frozen in time. It was definitely an attractive place to live, with forests, lakes, pastiche Dutch houses and Frederick the Great's strikingly

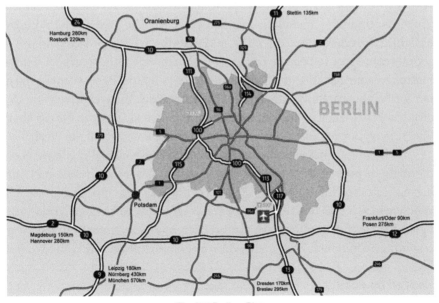

The A10 Berliner Ring

61

yellow, ageing summer palace Sanssouci. In commercial property terms, however, fairy-tale Potsdam felt too far away from Berlin to be of much significance, even if Potsdam-Babelsberg was known as the 'German Hollywood' – the film industry even attracted ambitious plans for a high-end mixed-use project by Elliott Bernerd's Chelsfield. However, Potsdam's planners proved too slow and ponderous for that scheme to fly.

Schönefeld, the former DDR's main airport, was the natural centre of gravity for business. The airport's junction on the Ring, Schönefelder Kreuz, led south to Dresden. Berlin's future mega-airport or *Großflughafen* was the subject of much speculation even in the early 1990s; every week the *Berliner Zeitung* and *Berliner Morgenpost* carried articles on the future airport.

Just as Berlin had multiple opera houses, there were multiple future airport options. It began with the three small airports at Tempelhof, Tegel and Schönefeld, but the government also considered other viable options which history had handed Berlin. When the Soviet Union finally left Germany, it left behind not only military hardware and pollution, but also a lot of prime real estate land. The Union of Soviet Socialist Republics had used no less than 3% of the country – including a working airport. The huge Soviet military airfield at Sperenberg was not far from the southern Berliner Ring and was a serious contender to become the *Großflughafen*. Sperenberg airport scored high on existing facilities and low on additional pollution, but was finally ruled out for being located too far south of the Ring. Back then, express trains to airports were a thing of the future and even Schönefeld, closer to the city than Sperenberg, just felt like a tiring journey from the comforts of the West.

As Ronnie Lyon's experience showed earlier, Schönefeld may have been the main airport of the East, but it was still so basic that it only had one luggage carousel. Like most of my friends at the time, I avoided flying through Schönefeld as Tegel and Tempelhof were so agreeably convenient. Today, the new BER (Berlin Brandenburg airport) sits in a field almost immediately adjoining Schönefeld. That great white elephant is physically complete but has not opened. Just as in the past, the local press carries a new article every week on the subject.

Around the Ring, many submissions for out-of-town development schemes were tabled. Briefly, there was a sudden, frenetic gold rush of urban planning. However, if negotiating the red tape of the planning process was difficult inside the city, it was also sometimes more complicated outside Berlin. The lack of regional vision and co-ordination between the governments of Land Berlin and Land Brandenburg meant the two states competed against each other for the benefits of commercial development, such as jobs and corporate taxes. In the prime stretch of the southern Berliner Ring, Land Brandenburg and Land Berlin respectively promoted business to the south and north of the ring road, and usually did so without speaking to each other.

Prime looking land there was plentiful – on paper anyway. Every motorway junction had abundant greenfield sites although, in practice, many were either contaminated or blocked by one of east Germany's 100,000 restitution claims. The property developers and military commanders of the USSR seemed to have a shared preference for the southern Berliner Ring with its easy access to Leipzig, Dresden and Warsaw. My East German colleague, Marc, knew from his connections that the Russian Army would be giving up a lot of big sites soon – and, mysteriously, he even knew exactly which ones. Many of these sites had been commandeered by the Soviets for the strategic quality of their locations. Unusually for a German, Marc had once seen the legendary '*Kleinmoskau*' – the town of Wünsdorf, on a lake close to the southern Ring. Over 50,000 Soviet citizens had lived here – in almost total isolation – since 1945. They even had a direct train line to Moscow. Soon those inhabitants would be going home and leaving a giant military junkyard in the hands of Land Brandenburg. Some of Wünsdorf's 700 buildings were said to have future potential and plans were floated to relocate public sector workers there.

Post-*Wende*, many sleepy small villages and farming communities near the southern Berliner Ring had caught the eye of the property pioneers. By the standards of Land Brandenburg, Wünsdorf was a relatively big town among little hamlets. The community I came to know best was the rural cluster of Genshagen, where the THA had a huge site for sale. They had been seeking a single investor with the skills and financial muscle to develop out and create thousands of jobs over the next decade. As always in Berlin at the time, it took a lot of imagination to see ten years ahead for the village of Genshagen (population ca. 600), which was distinguished mainly by a bucolic past, a thirteenth-century church, a crumbling castle and a sleepy *Gasthaus* called the *Goldener Eber* – golden boar.

Genshagen village triggered a memorable coincidence for me – a curious meeting of the past and the present. At the same time as I was in Berlin, my best man Angus was attached to the British Army in west Germany. One Friday night we travelled to a mess dinner attended by his father, Stuart (known affectionately as 'The Colonel') who had once been a 'spook' for Her Majesty's intelligence services in Germany. When the Colonel asked what was keeping me busy in Berlin, I described my job in generic high-level terms and mentioned the land where I was working on the Ring south of Berlin. The Colonel pressed for specific details and astounded me by volunteering that not only did he know Genshagen, but he had even spent time drinking in the *Gasthaus*. In the 1970s, Angus's father would have been drinking undercover, since for the British forces, the village would have been five miles on the 'wrong' side of the Wall. To my surprise, he was able to recall and name *Goldener Eber*. It was a 'heavy hand of history' Berlin moment, bringing together his past and my present.

The availability of this jumbo tract of land was partly the work of Gottfried Schindler, the mayor of Genshagen and partly a result of the THA breaking up the former DDR's collective farms. *Gute Grossbeeren* was one of the largest farms and the former head of that agricultural collective just happened to be mayor Schindler. In a paternal way, Schindler foresaw the coming tsunami of unemployment and the need to attract jobs for his citizens and former colleagues. Schindler later became a local hero for bringing relative prosperity to the village.

The THA organisation, the vendors at Genshagen, were the kings of the Berliner Ring in 1991 and 1992. For a short time, they were very powerful, running businesses that employed over four million staff and owning vast agricultural land holdings. As their liquidations caused huge unemployment, however, the THA were massively unpopular in some quarters. The head of the organisation was assassinated in his west German home because he was seen as flogging off east Germany too enthusiastically and expediently.

When buying land from the THA around the Ring, the prevailing question from my clients was to quantify who would use the road in the short, medium and long term. Office, retail and residential uses were all considered, but with demand rooted at the low-value end of the chain, the short-term answer lay in making things and storing things. That meant *Gewerbeparks*. Most out-of-town planning applications were in that sector, a high-density/ low-end cousin of the business park concept in the United States and UK. The use of these parks was mainly limited to low-value production/light industrial/warehouse with limited offices. Examples existed outside Frankfurt, Düsseldorf and Munich, but the *Gewerbepark* product had not yet made it as an institutional-grade investment. Given the plentiful long-term supply of land and the lack of coordination between the authorities of Berlin and Brandenburg, the parks were certainly easy to replicate around the Berliner Ring.

The competitive advantages of these greenfield sites in Land Brandenburg over Berlin's brownfield or urban sites were scale and simpler land ownership. The major disadvantages were the two recurrent legacies of the former DDR: dreadful access roads off the neglected Ring and reckless industrial and environmental pollution in the soil. For those private sector developers creating low-value industrial sites near the Ring, resolving these big environmental and infrastructure problems was rarely cost effective.

In the early 1990s, over 200 *Gewerbeparks* were proposed around the Ring. The vast majority never got to first base, but those that survived were split between parks adopting basic, local standards and a few which embraced international standards. Some publicly funded ventures enjoyed the luxury of subsidies and proved hard to beat for private sector developers, both local and international.

Public funding produced winners like the *Güterverkehrszentrum* (GVZ or freight centre) at Grossbeeren on the Ring. That Grossbeeren GVZ had two key advantages: favourable tax breaks for occupiers and proximity to an intermodal capacity, with access to the Teltow canal, linking up the two key hubs to the south of the city – Potsdam and Schönefeld.

This waterway was the subject of a memorable on-site exchange between Ronnie Lyon and a clueless local broker in a smart mustard jacket. Bored by the broker's overlong sales pitch, a curious and playful Ronnie watched freight barges steaming past on the canal and asked:

"So, where, exactly, do these boats come from, and where are they travelling to?"

The agent, not wanting to admit his obvious ignorance, put on a solemn face and replied:

"Ach, Mister Lyon, you know... here and there..."

Ronnie's caustic sense of humour sensed an opportunity.

"Oh, I see. And what, exactly, are the boats carrying when they go here and there?"

"Ach Mister Lyon, you know... this and that..."

From that day, both in our own office and in any conversation with Ronnie Lyon, "zis and zat" became an insider euphemism for not understanding. In 1993, there was a lot of "this and that" because if the standard of property advice in the city was poor, then the market for flogging land around the Berliner Ring was worse. For the new Weatheralls business, the mustard jackets of the Ring were a business opportunity. For a time, we were the one-eyed man in the kingdom of the blind.

The clear jewel amongst the many would-be *Gewerbeparks* was at Dreilinden, occupying the site of the former Checkpoint Bravo. This iconic location, though less famous than Checkpoint Charlie, had a special place in the hearts and minds of Germans. Like Charlie, Bravo had a collection of tragic-heroic Cold War stories of wall crossings – such as the tale of three-year old Holger, accidentally suffocated by his mother as she tried to smuggle him across to the west in the boot of a truck.

In 1993, French investor Europarc bought the Dreilinden site and planned for a long-term future of mixed uses. The site had lots going for it:

great visibility from a major *Autobahn* and proximity to business in the western city centre, current and future. It was also close to Tegel airport and next door to the wealthy residential areas of Zehlendorf and Grünewald which could, on paper, feed future demand from higher-value uses such as retail and leisure.

Godfrey Bradman and Ronnie Lyon assembled a huge *Gewerbepark* site at Königs Wusterhausen, close to Schönefelder Kreuz. With the help of their well-connected and capable lawyer, Andreas Plesske, they contracted land options with over 40 small owners. Deutsche Telekom's training centre signed up as the first major occupier at Königspark, but little else followed, despite that blue-chip anchor. The land prices there were simply unaffordable for low-value users.

The *Gewerbepark* losers included big German names like Mercedes. The historic IFA site at Ludwigsfelde on the southern Ring had manufactured Luftwaffe aircraft engines in World War II and then scooters and trucks in the DDR. The site had been sold by the THA to Mercedes, but post-purchase, the buyers did not follow through on their contractual commitments. It triggered a considerable scandal when the mighty Daimler-Benz reneged on their much-lauded real estate plans, even if Mercedes did continue making trucks and creating jobs there.

By 1993/94, other German investors were beginning to take the same expedient and cynical attitude to commitments made only three years earlier. At the THA, this caused ripples of worry – if a German household name could pull the plug, would others from overseas follow them out of the door?

The THA looked again at the credibility of its international partners and investors, which included the largest landowner on the Ring, Horsham Properties from Canada. The THA had sold them their huge *Gewerbepark* site at Genshagen – right opposite Daimler Benz at Ludwigsfelde. Luckily for the local economy, Horsham kept to the spirit of their agreement. With the help of Coca-Cola, the pioneering Canadians would prove true to their word.

7 PIONEERS IN THE PARK

THE dictionary definition of a pioneer is "a person who is among those who first enter or settle a region, thus opening it for occupation and development by others". On the blank page of the Berlin property industry, Canada's Horsham Group were a pioneer's pioneer. They ventured beyond the real estate world of urban Berlin and into the green fields of sparsely populated and impoverished Land Brandenburg. The comfort blankets of the real estate profession are plenty of people, plenty of buildings, plenty of public transport and plenty of capital. This was pioneering without blankets. Germany's five *neue Bundesländer* out beyond the Berliner Ring were uncharted territory where few rational investors dared to tread. Horsham positioned themselves on these outer fringes of the investor universe. Their Brandenburg Park was not located at the end of the universe, but you could certainly see it and touch it from there.

It was hard to be a pioneer breaking the Berlin mould. Peter Sidebottom, a board member of Horsham Europe, remarked on how advisors and consultants, having gathered precious knowledge from Horsham at Brandenburg Park (BP), were regularly picked off to employ that experience with Horsham's various competitors. Sidebottom volunteered the old wisdom: "You know what they say about pioneers? All they get is arrows in their backs!"

The Horsham Group had strong personalities at the helm. Peter Munk was a self-made billionaire with pioneering DNA who had made his fortune mining gold in Canada and had proven property skills, having developed hotels in Asia. Crucially, as a Hungarian emigré in the war, he felt sufficiently at home to be amongst the very first to return to invest in *Mitteleuropa* when the Iron Curtain fell.

He hired flamboyant developer Iain Shearer to run his European business in Berlin. The charismatic Shearer had been involved with Stockley Park next to Heathrow Airport, the benchmark for high-end business parks. Iain, a Scottish entrepreneur of conviction, was determined to replicate that model outside Berlin. At an initial meeting with Coca-Cola, Iain explained Brandenburg Park's site plan on the wall in Horsham's office. As we left to drive down there, he added absent-mindedly that he knew they would enjoy visiting "Stockley Park". Iain was convinced that Horsham would concentrate on building out the 210 hectares and selling investment properties. Moreover, those investments would be mostly let to high-end offices for users such as IBM and Hewlett Packard. He was sniffy about flogging plots of land and dismissed the Coca-Cola sale as "a soft deal" – a loss-leading transaction to tee up the real business of building out and letting speculative offices. Shearer did not last: following a difference of opinion with Horsham head office in Toronto, he left the company. The deal with Coke and the departure of Shearer were to set the Canadian pioneers on a more conservative and ultimately successful path.

Prior to Brandenburg Park, Horsham had planted a flag in the Berlin market, which accelerated the site acquisition. The City of Berlin had ruffled feathers in the west Berlin property cartel (known as the *Betonmafia*) by surprisingly nominating Horsham as the investor for the high-profile Jannowitzbrücke redevelopment in the East district of Berlin-Mitte. In the old pre-*Wende* days, the small inner circle of Berlin players was accustomed to carving up subsidised public tender business without internationals barging in. Horsham did not end up developing Jannowitzbrücke (which was sold to Allianz a few years later), but having proved a certain commitment and credibility, they had put themselves on the THA's radar.

The THA, the vendors of Genshagen, were pioneers like Horsham. They received arrows in the back which more than once proved to be for real – such as the 1991 murder of *Treuhand* chief executive Detlev Rohwedder in his west German residence. Closer to home, in the world of Berlin real estate, 48 year-old Hanno Klein, the *Baubeamte des Senats* (Senate official responsible for construction), was killed by a letter bomb later the same year. Klein bled to death overnight in his study in Wilmersdorf. He was responsible for promoting foreign investment and had dealt with all the heavyweight international investor/developer names. Both Sidebottom and Shearer had met Klein – who was thought of as the 'eye of the needle' for an international like Horsham wanting to get on the Berlin map with a major project.

This second assassination was an uncomfortable moment for those of us working in Berlin's fledgling industry. Rumours flew. Though the Russian Mafia were instantly under suspicion, the educated guess in Horsham's office was that the *Betonmafia* probably had its fingerprints on that fatal device. It was thought to be a bungled warning shot, because the short-sighted Klein was not wearing his glasses and was peering closely at the unfamiliar A5 envelope. Whatever the origins and motivations of the attack, the shock waves rippled out to foreign investors, who became uncomfortably aware of personal security. Philip Jones, MD of Horsham Berlin, can recall being instructed on how to use a mirror on a stick to look for explosive devices under his family car. As with some other curiosities in those pioneering days, Philip did not share that lesson with his wife Jane.

Bombs or no bombs, Horsham were definitely the target of hostility from the west Berlin real estate cartel for occupying their long-held territory. Against this background, the advice of city mayor Eberhard Diepgen's team was for Horsham to set its sights on less high-profile properties than in Mitte, such as the THA's 210-hectare site at Genshagen. Most of the land further north was contaminated, having been used as open sewage fields, so it was uniquely appropriate for large-scale development.

Horsham's acquisition carried the important condition that they had to enter an irrevocable commitment to create jobs, develop the whole site and build out the infrastructure. The THA/Horsham sale negotiations proved complex because no one really knew what would or could happen next. Job creation was the state's natural priority, so it was curious that the THA had wanted to contractually exclude third-party investments – which would have prevented simple land sales to future occupiers such as Coca-Cola (whose major investment alone later created almost 200 jobs).

In the purchase contract, the DM 21 million (€10.8 million) had to be paid upfront. The price of DM 10 per m² appeared low on paper but the site was, in practice, no more than unzoned agricultural land. The main source of comfort to the buyer was the stated commitment of Land Brandenburg to see the land zoned – one day. After purchase, Horsham's new team of planning specialists

PROPERTY

Horsham fights its way past German red tape

Cutting through the jungle usually took a decade

chuckled when their clients explained that it was the state's intention to grant zoning sometime, especially in the context of a western planning system which had, naturally, never been road tested in the former DDR. They explained that, in Germany, obtaining outline *Bebauungsplan* zoning is a long and painful municipal process to be performed ahead of building permits and that cutting through the jungle of red tape typically took a decade.

Horsham briefly felt the discomfort of the dynamic pioneer, that in boldly rushing ahead of the pack they had, unwittingly, overpaid for what instinctively felt like cheap land. In the end, it was the pioneering developers and not the sceptical lawyers who got that call right. The zoning of Genshagen actually took 18 months, not 120.

Horsham's trick in accelerating that zoning process was to overlay a large and privately funded team onto the Genshagen village administration. A few previous administrators of the collective farm system were engaged to navigate a highly contrived municipal path through the West German planning system. They had the assistance of Land Brandenburg, but their motivation visibly flagged the moment they announced that they had secured Horsham as a foreign investor.

Brandenburg Park in 1995

Like all groundbreaking pioneering schemes, Horsham's Brandenburg Park left a legacy to the industry. In their purchase deeds, the park's new occupiers were required to sign up for a ten-year maintenance contract that defined green zones and tightly regulated what private owners could and could not do. By the standards of the basic German market, this was visionary.

One of the main legacies of Brandenburg Park later widely adopted by the industry was the simple roundabout. *Verkehrskreiseln* are commonplace in Germany today, but were an innovation at the time. For forward-looking municipalities, Brandenburg Park was an early reference point and the Brandenburg authorities later fell in love with the capacity of roundabouts to deal with high-capacity junctions. High-quality landscaping was also unfamiliar territory in Germany. Even if lakes on an industrial park were an appealing novelty for users, the single most distinguishing design feature of the park was actually the micro-location of the compulsory green areas. German zoning law required 20% of the plot to be green, but before Brandenburg Park it was allocated randomly. Horsham created continuous bands at the front and back of each plot.

Lastly, Horsham was the first *Gewerbepark* investor prepared to commit major funds to marketing and hire full-time employees solely for that purpose.

Brandenburg Park's marketing story was underpinned by a pair of unique factors: the association with the massive Coca-Cola brand and the emotional draw of the story of Peter Munk, the prodigal son from *Mitteleuropa*. Those stories were duly amplified by the unprecedented scale of the marketing campaign and the recycling of Horsham's PR team from the

Horsham's marketing was on an unprecedented scale
Jacques Delors and Philip Jones at the opening
ceremony of Brandenburg Park

political rezoning exercise. Jacques Delors, then president of the European Commission, was at the opening ceremony to highlight both the political importance of the huge scheme and its international dimension.

The external marketing campaign encountered plenty of challenges and Weatheralls was a major player in that team. Signing up Coca-Cola was a fine start for us but the momentum did not instantly translate into other successes. In 1993, post-*Wende* euphoria in the Berlin economy was starting to cool off.

73

German companies tended to view the Coke transaction with suspicion as an insider deal between North American groups.

We searched for international business park reference points to help sell Horsham's land to occupiers. Prospective tenants were even flown out to the upscale Sophia Antipolis Park in Nice, France's best-known equivalent. The reality at Genshagen was, of course, much more modest than Sophia Antipolis or Stockley Park in London Heathrow. The land next to the village of Genshagen was neither next to one of the world's biggest airports, and nor did it benefit from a soft year-round climate, rolling hills, golf courses, palm trees or a view of the Cote d'Azur.

In parallel to our external marketing, Horsham also ran a public relations campaign designed to win political approval. Winning hearts and minds was commercially vital if we were to add value to the land Horsham had just purchased and stay ahead of the chasing pack. With the states of Berlin and Brandenburg competing to grant planning permissions, it was key to get into the market promptly and pass on Horsham's trump card of low acquisition cost to the users of the land.

Horsham's public relations machine delivered the administrative and voting results required to navigate that red tape in record time. The PR team set out to align the interests of the villagers with those of Horsham and included crucial little personal touches – Philip Jones's daughter, for example, attended the Genshagen village kindergarten. One day, a well-meaning colleague (who had grown up and been educated in East Berlin) took Jones to one side:

"Philip – you cannot send your daughter to this school."

"Why not? It's working fine?"

"Because, Philip, these people are rural peasants..."

Horsham made various promises in that hearts and minds PR campaign; they persuaded other villages to help support the tiny local administration and prioritise Genshagen's need for financial and legislative support. At the same time, they provided administrative jobs in the village of Genshagen itself and brought in businesses to the Park which would generate a lot of employment in the village.

They also undertook to deliver some major environmental measures – such as draining wetland areas and diverting water courses away from houses. Horsham funded water supply for the villagers – although in practice, this was something of a 'Trojan Horse' in order to be able to supply essential water to Coca-Cola and the rest of the Park. Lastly, they sponsored the supply of paint and flower boxes for citizens to cheer up their scruffy housing, a promise which backfired at one point and led to accusations of Horsham bribing the villagers.

Although that PR 'hearts and minds' campaign was beginning to work well, the fizz temporarily went out of the sales campaign after the launch of Coca-Cola. It took over a year for the next deal to be struck with a west Berlin metal fabricator called ALMO – and that for only half a hectare. Finally, after we had signed up five or six contracts, we had the feeling that the project was really going to fly. By early 1995, as I left Berlin, 30 users had signed up for almost 50 hectares, creating over 1,000 jobs. The village of Genshagen provided much of that workforce.

Despite Peter Sidebottom's misgivings and the occasional arrow in the back, pioneering Horsham finally ended their quest by arriving in the promised land. Getting ahead of the competition had been all about speed and timing. Speed counted and allowed them a good return on cash when they sold out in 2001.

In tricky times, Horsham had bought low and bought early. They snagged a big fish of a user ahead of the competition, then applied huge resources to lever up that catch and attract many others. When things got tough, the Canadian giants were also able to mobilise a lot of cash to avoid servicing expensive debt.

At the very edge of the investable universe, Horsham had succeeded in exploring and exploiting the grey fields of Land Brandenburg. By the dictionary definition of 'opening it for occupation and development by others', our Canadian client proved to be an outstanding pioneer.

8   THE REAL THING

COCA-COLA was one of Berlin's biggest success stories of the early 1990s. My small part in that success started with a routine cold call and ended up with the company building a plant that produced over a million bottles each week and anchored Berlin's premier business park for over 20 years. My Coca-Cola story is emblematic of those unique times.

The compelling backstory is important to recall. In the eleven months between the opening of the Wall and reunification, the initial spike in consumer demand from the former DDR had been for bananas and cola – two hard-to-get trophies of Western life – and specifically Coca-Cola. Fuelled by their DM 100 'welcome money', consumers sought out fast food. McDonald's and Burger King threw resources and energy at the new East German opportunities, but where the pace of fast food growth was constrained by the shortage of suitable outlets, fizzy drinks had far fewer distribution bottlenecks.

Vending machines simply sprang up faster than restaurants.

The story of how cold Coke stole the East German market has become a business school case study. The historical context is that the mighty Coca-Cola was experiencing challenging times in the 1980s. The Pepsi Challenge had successfully destabilised the red brand leader in its home markets, as consumers in blind tests decided that a sip of Pepsi tasted better than a sip of Coke. Coca-Cola objected that drinking a whole bottle of sweet Pepsi (as opposed to sipping it) would be a very different experience. Whatever the technicalities, the result was a dip in Coke's sales and a strategic win for the brand enemy. This setback prompted the disastrous 1985 introduction of 'New Coke' alongside the existing 'Classic Coke'. Tampering with the successful product had sapped a monumental amount of Coke's time, energy and resources.

In the late 1980s, Coke was conceding ground not only to the big blue competitor but also to determined retailers such as Carrefour and Metro. Furthermore, just as Coke's position was being eroded in its traditional base of North America and Western Europe, the company was failing to break in to new growth markets. In India they had even walked away from market leadership after being ordered by the Indian government to share Coke's 'secret formula' with a local JV partner. Proud of its corporate principles, Coca-Cola's head office in Atlanta stuck to its credo and refused to comply, a difficult commercial decision in a hot country with 800 million thirsty citizens. Coke remained absent from India between 1977 and 1993.

Towards the end of the 1980s, Coca-Cola was thus a stable dividend stock for investors but a little short of the magic potion of growth. In this context, the sudden collapse of Communism was a defining moment which changed the rules of the game, not just in Germany and Europe but around the world.

Surprisingly, Pepsico already had a toehold both in the DDR and other Central European communist countries. In 1959, Richard Nixon famously gave Nikita Khrushchev a taste for the stuff in Moscow in the televised Capitalism v Communism 'kitchen debate'. Pepsi was, in fact, the first foreign product to be legally approved for sale in the USSR. Bottling commenced in Moscow in 1972 and like a number of Cold War products, what worked well in the Soviet Union eventually filtered through to consumers in East Germany. The Russian cola, however, was said to taste oddly different from Pepsi in the USA.

In the early 1990s, Pepsi's foothold in East Berlin ended up working to Coke's advantage, precisely because East Germans had already tasted and disliked the rival product. Pepsi's problem was more practical than ideological. A bigger issue than the negative associations with the occupying Russians was the absence of fridges. Just as there were few telephones in East Germany, there were few ways of chilling a product which tasted sickly when lukewarm. To many Easterners, 'cola' meant either the DDR's saccharine 'Vita Cola' or warm Pepsi's too-sweet taste of cloyed caramel. I knew that to be true as I had sipped warm Pepsi in the DDR from a peculiar-looking bottle on a hot day in East Berlin's Treptow Park in May 1988. It was memorably awful.

Seven weeks before the end of the 1980s the momentum shifted – out of the blue – in what John Pilger later christened the 'Ice Cold War' between Pepsi and Coke. On that Thursday night in November 1989, when holes unexpectedly appeared in the Berlin Wall, Paul-Gerhard Ritter, head of the Berlin depot of Coca-Cola, whistled up delivery trucks from Lichterfelde to the fresh gaps in the border. As Easterners swarmed into West Berlin for their very first glimpse of freedom, a free 'welcome-to-the-west' Coca-Cola was pressed into their hand. There were cases of Coke for those travelling in Trabant cars and six-packs for visitors on foot. By the end of that wild night, hundreds of thousands of red-branded free drinks had been distributed to a new market. Ritter had seized the day. The symbolism, always of importance in the Cola Wars, was huge: red Coke was the drink of the free and the drink of the future. Suddenly, nobody in the old East wanted blue Pepsi-Cola, which became by association the taste of repression and a monochrome, no-choice past.

Momentum built swiftly. Within weeks, Coca-Cola made the courageous policy decision to accept Ostmarks at 1:1 to the Deutschmark. With a black market rate at 4:1 or 5:1, Coke's bet on early currency unification was bold, because even in early 1990 a final unification date seemed distant. The

78

ultimate 1:1 exchange rate also looked improbable. Coke's gamble was to prove the right call in winning hearts and minds and captured a huge future market share. In the coming months, fridges – often second-hand from the West – steadily became available throughout the East to reinforce the fresh (and chilled) taste of freedom. The dismantling of East Germany proceeded at a rapid pace, with the currencies uniting on July 1 prior to full reunification on October 3.

"all your daily needs" Cans of Coca-Cola arrive in an East Berlin corner shop in 1990 *(photo: Gerd Danigel)*

Coca-Cola's German management, backed by head office in Atlanta, understood this moment was the chance of a lifetime. Speed was of the essence and *Carpe Diem* was the credo. Coca-Cola Germany outflanked Pepsi to buy the half dozen bottling plants available across the former DDR from the *Treuhandanstalt*. They rebranded the bricks and mortar and retrained the 2,000 staff. Human resources were also poured across from West Germany and exhorted by country manager Heinz Wiezorek to spare no energy. Coke's resourceful staff adapted to overcome the real hurdles of infrastructure in the five new states. As there were few hotels, Coke reps slept overnight in their cars as they dashed to capture outlets. Old-fashioned

25 Jahre
MAUERFALL
Wie die Coke
einfach rüberflog

A successful marketing image from 1990 – part of the recent 25-year reunification celebrations

telegrams were sent ahead to organise meetings and deliveries, since there were no faxes or mobiles and few telephone lines. Coke's new 'red army' improvised distribution channels at the counters of hotel bars and stacked vending machines and coke fountains into prestigious East German icons such as Berlin's huge Sports Hall.

Marketing power amplified the successful surge. The iconic advertisement of an East German border guard on top of the Wall was a prominent example. The uniformed soldier was clasping a red can and the slogan: "*Wirf mir auch was mal rüber*" ("just throw one over to me") captured the unique *Zeitgeist*. TV advertisements ran and ran with dynamic attractive people dancing to the jingle "You can't beat the real thing". The searing hot weather of 1992, my first summer in Berlin, poured fuel on that fire. Thirsty people drank Coke and felt thirsty for more.

It was against that background of straining production capacity and overstretched supply chains that my own Coke story began. As a young agent marketing plots of land on Horsham's jumbo business park on the Berliner Ring, I was tasked with testing out user demand for the client in the traditional way: cold calling. My German vocabulary was enriched by a couple of weeks spent trawling a semi-filtered list of companies from the phone book. For a graduate in German literature, these constant phone rejections were a hard lesson. As seen earlier, the real estate *Makler* had a very low standing in German business culture and the sharp responses to my unsolicited calls on the telephone were not in the poetic language of Goethe. By the time I had got as far as the letter 'C', I was starting to get used to the cold shoulder. So I was surprised when the person responsible for property expansion at Coca-Cola Berlin, Hans-Joachim Klötz, expressed what sounded like genuine interest in the product we were offering. On the telephone, he had a distinctive East German lilt and came over as intelligent and approachable. He was not just interested in the product I was selling but curious about my unusual accent and our office address at Unter den Linden, a place with rich emotional clout for East Germans.

As ever at that time, the story of the characters in the deal was intriguing. Herr Klötz was a product of Coca-Cola's newly acquired bottling businesses in the former East. The problem for Coca-Cola's management was finding enough Klötzes in the former DDR, where the laws of supply and demand and open-market economics were a foreign language. Klötz was one of the most gregarious and driven of the new recruits and had been sent on a crash course in capitalism in the West. He and I developed a good business relationship but never broke the respectful linguistic and social barrier of the polite '*Sie*' form. I gradually realised he conversed very differently with our East German office manager who met up with him out of the office. They addressed each other with the familiar '*du*' form and it was clear they had a strong cultural link which I would never fully understand. When off-the-record deal messages needed passing, the special bond of the East was a valuable channel of communication.

Dr Horst Müller, Herr Klötz's charismatic boss, was a West German and in charge of Coke's German expansion. Within Coca-Cola, the Doktor was known as the driving force behind the recyclable plastic bottle (*Mehrwegflasche*). He had the backing of head office to invest in the East wherever the cause of expansion required it. For that brief time, the Americanised German was the golden boy of Atlanta and had their full confidence to act swiftly and without the straightjacket of risk management. When Dr Müller drove out with us to the ring road to see Horsham's land, we realised Herr Klötz's interest was for real. Coca-Cola started to get to know Horsham as the developer of the big project and put into action their mantra to 'think global and act local'. Globally, there was a good cultural fit between the respective North American head offices in Atlanta and Toronto. Locally, Herr Klötz discovered through the former DDR grapevine that he had many shared experiences with Horsham's legal counsel, Reinald Walkemeyer. Both were English-speaking East Germans living in Hohenschönhausen who had been permitted to travel and who had received some special training in Moscow. They, too, developed a special relationship based on a shared knowledge of the way things had been done in the DDR.

From his Hohenschönhausen office in east Berlin, the daily pre-occupations of Herr Klötz were *a)* that the Coca-Cola bottling plant in Dunkirk was overloaded with demand from east Germany and *b)* that the supply chain from France was overstretched. Coca-Cola in west Germany was still fundamentally a collection of fragmented family businesses, but in northern France, Coke owned 100% of the big state-of-the-art plant and had been able to swiftly accelerate production there. Nevertheless, the beaches of Dunkirk, 900 km away, were a long, long truck journey from Berlin and 16 million thirsty East Germans. Herr Klötz needed a new large-scale production facility in Germany, preferably in the East, on the doorstep of the future new clients in the region. The land I was selling for Horsham had plenty of scale for Coke's ten-hectare requirement and was located only an hour from Poland and a further 40 million potential customers.

To better understand their production requirement, Herr Klötz took me to a small existing facility for Coca-Cola and Fanta, the group's citrus product, a German invention in wartime when they ran out of American cola syrup.

Challenged to use their *Fantasie* (imagination) to come up with a name for the new *ersatz* product, the management of the time decided on "*Fanta!*" My visit to the plant's aromatic vats of bubbling sugary liquid was a thought-provoking slice of life, making immediate to me the scale of the future operation and the importance of Atlanta's 'secret formula', known only to a handful of top Coke executives in the world.

Our big property deal began to take shape as a simple land purchase. Both sides were feeling their way on pricing: quite simply, there had never been a remotely comparable transaction of serviced land in east Germany. It was more of a question of costing the final product and working backwards. The ten-hectare deal was struck at DM 180 per m² (€95 per m²) – incidentally, not far from today's quoting levels at Brandenburg Park.

There were mutual benefits for both Toronto and Atlanta. For Horsham in Toronto, there was, naturally, a major first mover advantage to having a world-class name on the *Gewerbepark* before the tap of rezoned industrial land opened to flood the out-of-town-market. Even more pressing than that long-term credibility was Horsham's short-term need for cash flow. Philip Jones, the British MD of Berlin, had clear instructions from Toronto that the local Horsham business was to turn the agricultural land into business land by working through the politics and financing the infrastructure. In doing so, Toronto insisted that the German office would get no head office subsidies in funding estate roads, landscaping, water and electricity. In a 'chicken and egg' financing situation, Coca-Cola fortunately proved to be a flexible and cash-rich player. In negotiations, Jones was able to undertake to deliver most things to Coca-Cola – as long as they paid DM 18 million (€9.5 million) upfront for their 100,000 m² of serviced land.

Coca-Cola's main preoccupations were twofold: image and water. Even though they were acknowledged by Atlanta as necessary to the *Carpe Diem* dash for growth, the random war-vintage bottling plants in east Germany were poorly configured and inconsistent with the company's multinational image. Head office wanted a model piece of real estate to show off to consumers and business partners in the new German states as well as to those in future markets further to the East. They also saw a chance at Brandenburg Park to create international-grade property, in line with what they operated in Rio, London, Paris or at home in Atlanta.

Image was important but the search for water was the number one deal imperative for Coca-Cola. It took nearly three litres of water to produce a litre of Coke, so a guaranteed supply was a functional necessity. Horsham could not guarantee a supply of pure drinking water, even if Berlin sat on marshy wet ground. Teams from Coca-Cola and Horsham joined up to attend Land Brandenburg water conferences and work out a pragmatic solution. Coca-Cola's future workforce was the village of Genshagen and as part of the 'hearts and minds' PR campaign, Horsham would provide funding for the village water supply to the local authority's *Wasser-zweckverband*. This supply, incidentally, had enough capacity for the whole business park and a four-line bottling plant for Coca-Cola.

The unusual and very East German hurdle in the way of providing that water was the *Rieselfelder* (sewage fields). East Berlin's untreated sewage had been liberally sprayed on the agricultural fields around Genshagen without a thought for tomorrow. In 1992, many greenfield development sites around Berlin were, quite literally, in the shit. Curiously, a lot of the places where raw sewage had been dumped turned out to be just over kinks in the line of the Wall which just happened to be near high-density west Berlin suburbs such as Lichtenrade. The contamination at Brandenburg Park was successfully managed down over time with more sewage, so that the enzymes in the earth would not contaminate the water table or destroy the roots of the many pine trees.

After our big Coca-Cola land deal was finally signed early in 1993, the really emblematic part of the story was what happened next. Namely, nothing. It took several years for Coca-Cola to build out the intended production facility, since their estimates of production had been based on exponential growth in the heady, energetic period after reunification. When the froth settled, it became clear that the extra production capacity would not be needed until demand picked up in other former Eastern Bloc countries. That happened almost ten years later and after a restructuring of the Coke business.

In the meantime, the inflated production estimates were treated as a state secret in case Pepsi found out. For the rest of the century, very little moved on Coke's ten hectares of land. By the time the people of Genshagen were producing bottles of Coke, Horst Müller, the golden boy of Atlanta, had left Coca-Cola.

In retrospect, this story followed a very Berlin real estate pattern. The high-energy sprint immediately post-*Wende*, followed by a decade of inaction, was like the office market (see the postscript chapter *The Tale of the Retail Tortoise and the Office Hare*). It was a similar story too in the residential market in the Berlin region, where values eroded steadily from 1994 to 2007.

The big Coca-Cola deal, notwithstanding the time lag, launched the long-term future of Brandenburg Park, the backbone of income for my company's growing office. For Weatherall Green & Smith, for Horsham Properties and for the people of Genshagen, my cold call to Coca-Cola had turned out to be The Real Thing.

Part Three

LOOKING BACK

THEN AND NOW (1)
– INSIDE BERLIN

H INDSIGHT is always 20/20 vision, allowing the reader to draw a lot of conclusions and say a lot of clever things after the event. That was not, however, the Berlin I once knew. For that reason, I have, up to now, tried to use hindsight sparingly in telling this story. My aim has been to capture the sense of wonder of that era, the sense of frenzied, nervous excitement, the sense of being on the front line.

The next two chapters will compare then and now, not from the wide perspective of history but through the narrower lens of real estate. This section will look at the buildings and locations from earlier in this book – the places where I spent my days between 1992 and 1994. Seen from today's vantage point, the chapters describe how those buildings and their micro-locations have changed – and try to tease out what that might say about the intervening years. Before looking at the buildings, however, it is important to put in context what it felt like 'then' and in particular the sense of wonder we had at the time.

As I started work in September 1989, I had no idea that within months the Iron Curtain would disappear or that Apartheid would end in South Africa. Telescoping these two once-in-a-generation events into a few weeks only amplified the sense of wonder. Either side of Christmas, free citizens of the DDR walked past border guards into West Berlin and a free Mandela walked past his prison guards.

For a short time, there was a feeling that anything could happen.

In August 1991, Mikhail Gorbachev was ousted by hardline Communists in the brief Soviet *coup d'état*. For three days, the world held its breath and watched pictures of tanks parked in Red Square. At about this time in west Berlin, Stuart Reid was awakened in his house by very loud metallic screeching noises. He was, briefly, convinced on waking that the Russian tanks (and there were very many stationed in Berlin) were rolling and the world was about to change just as radically as it had changed less than two years before. With the benefit of today's retrospective vision, that sounds a bit of a stretch but at the time, dear reader, anything felt possible. Stuart was, by the way, neither delusional nor a timid personality.

A personal anecdote from student days illustrates the firm certainties of 'then'. In May 1988, I toured the Berlin Reichstag with an Asian student who asked the standard harmless question about reunifying the two Germanies. The irritated Western lecturer snapped: "I wish people would stop wasting my time with this ridiculous question. Not in my lifetime!"

In hindsight, a historian can pull together the threads of how the Wall was coming down. We now know that Gorbachev encouraged *perestroika* and *glasnost* precisely because his old system was wobbling at home. At the time, however, it felt as if change could only come with violent bloodshed. In the 1950s, East Berliners protesting against long working hours had been gunned down by Soviet tanks on Karl-Marx-Allee. The Socialist Party in the DDR did not tolerate protests and in 1989, the Party was still made up of hardcore ideologues. As the Velvet Revolution was unfolding elsewhere, the DDR issued a policy statement: "Just because a neighbour changes his wallpaper does not mean you have to redecorate." This was not a joke. The Party did not do humour any more than it did protests. A doctor friend practising in East Berlin recalls how the big Charité hospital cancelled leave for medics and stocked up with very large quantities of blood in anticipation of a massacre at the huge Alexanderplatz freedom demonstration. That was five days before the Wall opened. It was, in hindsight, a close-run thing. That was then, the rest is now.

Scrolling ahead to today's central west Berlin, Uhlandstraße 14 (U14) remains a solid-looking building in a solid location. The small suites of offices are still multi-let to a variety of businesses, including a company called netdudes, a small representative of a fast-growing new tech sector in Berlin. The flag of the Embassy of Haiti now flutters from a new flagpole on the building – a reminder of an old Berlin phenomenon from my life in the 1990s. Looking up from the rear courtyard, you can see the Haitians and the netdudes still have the property's ugly, oversized radiators. In the cold winter of 1993, I would bleed those radiators in our show suite before viewings so that potential tenants would get a toasty let's-rent-this-space feeling. On completion in 1993, U14 was one of the best office properties in a city acutely short of quality buildings. Today, institutional-grade office constructions have proliferated in Berlin and highlight U14's limitations: the low ceiling heights, the noisy overhead train tracks and the absence of air conditioning.

Back then, the two U14 shops were let to a family of clothes retailers, the Borchardts, then a big retail name in Berlin, though more in the business of food than clothes. Five minutes after we had agreed the lease terms, Chris Bull-Diamond gave his opinion of the new retail tenant to our client Norwich Union: "That bloke won't last – he couldn't sell you a pair of socks." Chris was right. The Borchardts did not last – but they did help our client by investing in the expensive fitout of the U14 shop units. The current shop tenants – Breadleys café and a household goods unit – feel like appropriate long-term merchandising choices for the location. Nowadays, the U14 retail pitch is still cut off from the prime Ku'damm by the psychological barrier of the S-Bahn tracks overhead. The retail pitch, however, has been improved by the cafés and bistros under the rail track arches running to Savignyplatz. Those cafés were just taking root then, but now they are part of new Berlin's cultural furniture.

The most emblematic reflection of the new age of Berlin is the residential part of U14. New laws have promoted residential investment, and it shows. The residential area here used to be a mess. Now, the mosaic of small cobbled stones in the courtyard is well designed and well maintained. The tenant entrance halls are clearly delineated and attractive. Mature ivy has been trained to cover the plain concrete *Hinterhof* façade and looks inviting from the

The residential building to the rear of Uhlandstraße 14 – June 2016

street. The ivy has spread over the back of the office building and is starting to unify two very distinct buildings from different eras.

Google Earth confirms my recollection that the two respective buildings (office and residential) were about the same size. However, whereas in my time, the rent-controlled flats to the back only accounted for about 5-10% of the value, I guess that proportion may be as much as 30-40% today. Office rents have fallen as residential values have started to catch up.

In the wealthy western suburb of Steglitz, the Embassy of Thailand has fitted snugly into the leafy residential Lepsiusstraße. The arch of Waterglade's development showcases the classic stucco stone façade of the refurbished rear building, even if the new-build office to the front of the street looks utilitarian.

The Royal Embassy of Thailand, Berlin Steglitz – June 2016

In the gated courtyard, two flags fly proudly in front of three diplomatic vehicles with darkened glass windows. My former client, the Government of Thailand, sits in a neighbourhood which feels like a good example of the green space and mixed uses which remain so typical of Berlin.

Still in Steglitz, Kennet Carlsson's Birkbuschstraße 10 building once exemplified an emerging market trend to over-specify offices in weak office locations. Today, a *Jobcenter* stands on the large, luminous and efficient floor plates, as well as an air-conditioning system which was once ahead of its time. In hindsight, today's public sector occupier feels a more natural fit than private sector tenants such as EC Harris or an office furniture showroom. For today's jobseekers, the building's marble-clad entrance hall must feel a splendid welcome.

Meantime, Steglitz has been swamped with shopping centres. The prime retail drag of Schlossstraße has numerous galleries competing with each other, of which Klépierre/Corio's 87,000 m² Boulevard Berlin is only the latest and largest addition. In a city where planners have allowed shopping centres to become over-abundant in the last 25 years, Steglitz is a prominent example of micro-oversupply.

In nearby Friedenau, the location of our old flat in Wilhelmshöher Straße still looks like a classic slice of west Berlin. It is very attractive – and fundamentally little changed. The big building has been well maintained and still adjoins Pizzeria Cremina, our favourite cheap Italian trattoria on the corner of Südwestkorso. The tiny pizzeria still serves the same signature dish of tagliatelle with strips of peppered beef in cream sauce. Some of the same staff from that time still work there. The Mini Pizza, generously proportioned, has doubled in price, now costing one euro instead of one Deutschmark. Like so much in Berlin (both then and now), it still feels great value for money.

The ABC Tegel (Airport Bureau Center) was an example of a poor building in a poor office location. It still is. The big difference between now and then is the 'A' in Airport – and the very uncertain short-term future of west Berlin's remaining hub. The 50,000 m² property has been vacant for long spells over the last 25 years. The major occupier today is the low-cost

Air Berlin – but for how long? Like Tempelhof in 2008, Tegel is scheduled to close completely. In the meantime, with the fiasco of the still-to-be-opened BER airport, Tegel has crept up from processing seven million to seventeen million annual passengers.

The red tiled office buildings of the ABC are still surrounded by the charming low-rise allotments. In a very 'horizontal' location, the ABC building feels out of place and much too vertical. Even if the vegetable patches generate little traffic, the congestion on the Saatwinkler Damm is now very thick at peak times – partly because so many passengers are still driving in and out of Tegel each year. In the neighbourhood, there are still no S-Bahn or U-Bahn trains and very few lunch options for tenants. Just as for Tegel Airport's terminal, there will be no major investment in the fabric of the ABC building until the fog of political uncertainty has cleared.

In the centre of the former East, my old office has remained a little island of stability in a sea of activity – both in the reconstruction of the surrounding buildings and in the continued renewal of the infrastructure of Berlin-Mitte. Back then, Unter den Linden 12 had fine views over cranes swinging the length

Unter den Linden 12 – June 2016

of Friedrichstraße – at that time the biggest construction site in Europe. That construction is long completed but in its place there are now infrastructure works obscuring the avenue of famous *Linden* (lime) trees. The classy little building (if we overlook the little tourist shop selling Trabant knick-knacks) appears still to be in the ownership of the same private family office. The office tenants have now been diversified beyond the real estate industry and in the rear courtyard, I imagine the bullet holes may even have been filled in.

To the end of Unter den Linden, the new-look, pedestrian-friendly Pariser Platz pulls visitors past the immense Russian Embassy towards the

Brandenburg Gate. To the East, the Royal Palace is being rebuilt "for cultural purposes". One East-facing facade will recall Erich Honecker's glass-fronted 'lamp shop', demolished in 2008. The other three facades will be in the old baroque style. When complete, the huge palace will shift the centre of gravity down UDL towards Alexanderplatz.

At Checkpoint Charlie, where Liz used to clock in at the bank, the area now feels tawdry and touristy. In the early 1990s, this location still felt powerful and heavy with history. The nearby Gendarmenmarkt, on the other hand, feels like a significant achievement of civic architecture. The area of Mitte has clearly once again become the uncontested "middle" of the unified Berlin, but UDL itself does not feel like a world-class location. Not yet. Once the construction work is complete, it should in principle prove to be a thing of glory, but since the early 1990s, the wounded Berlin has been a constant work in progress. This is nothing new: a century ago, Karl Scheffler famously described Berlin as "condemned to always be the city that is forever going somewhere and never is".

To the northern end of Friedrichstraße, the iconic Tacheles squat is about to be redeveloped into upscale residential. As Berlin's centre of gravity for after-dark entertainment has shifted southwards towards Kreuzberg, the mad energy of Oranienburger Straße has been tamed. A line of multi-cultural shops and restaurants to the eastern end of the street leads into Rosenthaler Straße, where I once sublet 85 m² of grubby offices above a busy Burger King restaurant. Now it is home to Shusta, a boutique selling cool designer shoes. Where once were Whoppers is now the Bond Street of east Berlin, feeding off the recent strong growth in tourist trade. The Chamäleon theatre (the cabaret club where we saw the enigmatic Japanese mime artist) has remained in the Hackescher Markt, with its Berlin-signature *Hinterhöfe*.

In the Eastern districts near Mitte, gentrification is a very strong story, driven by new infrastructure. The Pankow of my colleague Regina, so grey and ugly on a dark February day in 1992, has become an attractive district with fine urban infrastructure: sleek trams, fast buses, handsome civic buildings and inviting shops.

The Prenzlauer Berg of my adventurous squash partner Peter has had an influx of wealthy newbies from west Germany. It is now much too comfortable and bourgeois to be an 'in' place. As gentrification radiates out from Mitte, its neighbour Friedrichshain is now one of the new affordable "hotspots" for Berlin's dynamic human capital. One measure is that the shops on the side streets here look as attractive as the main streets.

Further east in Lichtenberg, one wing of the former Stasi headquarters has been converted into a museum. The brown Paternoster lift is still there as an exhibit but no longer loops the loop. An upper floor has been retained in all its beige austerity. The lights are yellow, the phones beige, the desks light brown, the leather chairs dark brown. The net curtains, once white, seem to have faded to a light beige too. Schoolchildren see exhibits explaining how the Stasi targeted Iron Maiden and punk rockers as subversives. One picture looked a lot like Simon the goth, who was hauled off the bus at Checkpoint Alpha for his subversive behaviour with a sticker of Jürgen Klinsmann.

The rectangular appearance of the immediate surroundings of Lichtenberg has improved. The right angles have been softened by trees and wooden park benches but there is only so much that can be done between blocks of prefabricated concrete housing when they are 15 storeys high. The Karl-Marx-Allee still feels too wide and on an inhuman scale. One of the anomalies of the old DDR was that there were only four lanes on the motorways but six wide lanes of traffic on Karl-Marx-Allee – to facilitate large-scale military parades and allow tanks to move in swiftly to smash insurrections.

On this excursion to 'then and now', I left the city centre on Karl Marx's wide eastern boulevard and drove to the southern Berliner Ring, towards the two peculiar airports of Land Brandenburg.

10 THEN AND NOW (II) – OUTSIDE BERLIN

ARRIVING at Brandenburg Park on the southern Berliner Ring, I found Coca-Cola to be pleasingly present. In between the red-labelled delivery vans, the vehicles in the large and well-organised car park were mostly smart and German-made. Coca-Cola's head office in Atlanta would no doubt approve of the look of today's Brandenburg Park, where some small buildings are under construction for owner-occupiers. As a man jogged past in sports gear, I even felt there were some small hints of a North American style business park. Maybe it was just the sunshine and warmth of nostalgia.

The broad estate roads have good signage and fine roundabouts. The green landscaping feels well maintained. There are over 50 diverse occupiers encompassing pure logistics companies, Bavarian épicier Dallmayr, Scania trucks, a McDonald's and cheap hotels such as an Ibis Budget offering nights at €36. The two-star hotel has a TripAdvisor write-up which recommends the reader to "just stay, come and go" (but praises the breakfast). The smart Shell petrol station feels a bit over-dimensioned with a wide retail offer – the reason being there is no other real shopping on the park. The helpful staff were happy to exchange tales with me of Genshagen 25 years before. The McDonald's drive-thru was doing a brisk lunchtime trade, while the restaurant area inside was full of luminous yellow jackets from ADAC, the German Automobile Association. The Big Mac there still tasted like a Big Mac and, unlike in Leipzig in 1992, none of the east German customers needed to know the contents.

Coca-Cola production and storage facility, Brandenburg Park – September 2016

Despite the well-managed and consolidated feel of that older southern section, I did find myself wondering why there was not more at the location. With the exception of one jumbo logistics building, the huge north section has still not been built out.

From Brandenburg Park, I drove around the village of Genshagen itself, which, while not exactly prosperous, felt tidy and well presented, just like the park where the villagers have found jobs. Gottfried Schindler has done a good job watching out for his citizens, even if the 83-year-old is no longer mayor. The flowers are fresh in their boxes and most of the houses well-painted. The grass in front of the Goldener Eber was neatly cut. The façade of that modest *Gasthaus* (familiar to 'The Colonel' in the 1970s) displays no less than three Coca-Cola signs.

The village still definitely feels like the old East Germany – a good example is an old brick building with a DDR-style Friseur (hairdresser) sign to the main Genshagener Dorfstraße. As I stood trying to imagine an old East German hairdressing salon, a new Rolls-Royce swept past. It was an odd moment: the luxury car providing a bizarre cultural contrast which prompted me to think of my breakfasting experience in the fields of

Gasthaus 'Die Goldener Eber', Genshagen – September 2016

Land Brandenburg with Ronnie Lyon. Even after declaring a bankruptcy, Ronnie famously managed to drive around in a chauffeured Rolls – which explained why, when in a bad mood, he would complain about dawn drives in the passenger seat of my little Honda Civic and let me know I was "just a glorified chauffeur".

Googling Genshagen threw up a disturbing note which reflects a major issue in today's eastern Germany: immigration. A press article reported a knife fight between migrants, leaving six wounded, in Genshagen's *Asylantenheim* (refugee centre). It got me thinking about an elephant in the room – the relative absence of migrants in the city centre of Berlin. An informed insider later told me that the authorities of Berlin and Brandenburg have an (unpublicised) understanding that Land Brandenburg sweeps up most of the influx of migrants in return for subsidies. The abandoned buildings of what was once *Kleinmoskau* in Wünsdorf are now occupied by Syrians. Angela Merkel's gamble of bringing a lasting legacy of population growth to Germany has been punished by voters at local elections and will be tested at the general election in 2017. The immigration situation, as everywhere in Europe, remains the big issue of the day.

Looking at the slow growth of the location, the point, I surmised, is that for most of the years between then and now, Berlin's economy has been in bad shape. Since 1994, almost three million mobile and talented people have leaked away from east Germany. Now that good infrastructure has plugged the 'brain drain' in central Berlin, the deep wounds are healing – but that healing process is radiating out from the inside of the city. Berlin's population growth and recent recovery is mainly boosting the residential, retail and office sectors in the heart of the city centre. The global trend of urbanisation is also a headwind to Brandenburg Park. In 2015, for the first time since I left in 1994, the economies of the five *neue Bundesländer* grew as fast as those in the west – but since that growth is mainly in the cities, it will take time for the feelgood factor to seep out to peripheries such as the Berliner Ring in Land Brandenburg. The opening of the new airport (whenever that may be) would certainly help this macro location.

Further west at Dreilinden, the Europarc has consolidated near the upper end of the *Gewerbepark* scale. There are office buildings for Porsche and eBay and Autohaus car showrooms. Office buildings exist on several upper levels, with more under construction, but unlike the more industrial Brandenburg Park, they are seemingly being built on a speculative basis. The historic and threatening DDR watchtower at Dreilinden has been preserved. An eccentric Quadriga (like the famous four horses above the Brandenburg Gate) sits above a bank welcoming visitors to the city – something to do, I guess, with the weight of history at the former Checkpoint Bravo. Mad Berlin stuff.

Close to the Schönefelder Kreuz, Nobleclear's Königs Wusterhausen location has had an unexpected boost from the still-to-open BER airport, some 7 km away. When the entire village of Diepensee was expropriated to make room for a new runway, its 335 low-income citizens were all given brand new homes and new lives – in Königs Wusterhausen. They now live on the southern extremity of the Königspark site which Nobleclear assembled. After Ronnie died in 2004, it was his stepson, Michel Henri, who initiated those major negotiations with the city of Berlin.

Despite all this, industrial property at Königspark has never really taken off. Surprisingly, however, a giant regional shopping centre seems to have worked on land immediately opposite the Ring. A generation ago, no one was recommending retail development in the impoverished state of Brandenburg, let alone a big beast like the A10 centre.

The A10 is apparently one of the largest shopping centres in Germany (presumably measured in square metres rather than sales volume). A lot of land has been used, taken up by a Real hypermarket, Bauhaus and big boxes that add up to a mega regional dimension – on a single level. Tellingly, the sign on the entrance to the centre reads: "if you lift your eyes, you don't see the border". It felt curious to see the East/West border remains such a prominent topic all these years later. An information board by the toilets advertised tourist excursions in the Spreewald – where, since the Vetschau power station was shut in the mid-1990s, there are still gondoliers but no more smokestacks belching brown coal. Despite that splash of local colour and the reference to the border, there is little sense of place inside the shopping centre. The A10 could be an ECE-managed centre almost anywhere in Europe – in the Ruhrgebiet, on the ring road of Zaragoza or outside Wroclaw.

The A10 centre was acquired by the Otto family (the founders of ECE property management) in 2010 – not just to earn fees for their company's centre management but to make a return on their own invested capital. Given ECE's depth of data, that generally feels like a strong vote of confidence in the fundamentals of a German centre. Judging by what they wear and drive, the shoppers did not look wealthy. However, there were many visitors for a quiet period on a weekday, presumably coming from far afield and driving swiftly round the Ring. It made me think of the observation by the grandfather of the European shopping centre industry, the late Jean-Louis Solal, (sometimes known as "*le pape des centres commerciaux*" – the Pope of shopping centres), that retail malls are the 'Churches of the Poor'.

The new BER airport is a 15-minute drive from the A10 shopping centre. In the short term, the opening of the airport may not be a good thing for the shopping centre as it would finally launch the massive IKEA-anchored retail zone opposite the airport. Indirectly, however, the long-anticipated opening would stimulate jobs, homes and spending power to help the southern Berliner Ring prosper in the longer term.

Just as in the past, the density of traffic still tails off quickly to the eastern stretch of the Ring, although it now has six smoothly surfaced lanes and no potholes. The villages to the East mix the old and the new in a curious way. Ultra-modern tramways adjoin old houses and old churches next to new mini *Fachmarktzentren* (retail parks) with familiar discount traders like Schlecker and KiK.

Although the single luggage carousel at Schönefeld Airport has now become two carousels, Schönefeld, like Tegel, seems to be in a state of precarious limbo and is waiting for political certainty before investing heavily in the future. The official BER website says Schönefeld, today's low-cost hub, is being extended, but few Berliners any longer believe what the city says about airports.

BER itself, next to Schönefeld, is the great white elephant of our age. Its 360,000 m² of buildings occupy a site the size of 20 football fields. It feels like a disaster movie set in a Universal Studios theme park. The BER is one of the oddest things I have ever seen and is loaded with weird details: the express train from Leipzig to Berlin Hauptbahnhof stops at its 'ghost station', but the doors of the train do not open. Deutsche Bahn (DB) have to run some trains along the empty tracks to prevent moss forming in the tunnels. DB are suing the airport for non-use of their station.

The new BER airport, now empty for well over a thousand days

On the GPS of my hire car, the trace of the airport appeared on the screen, but with no street details, like a huge grey blob. The empty, flat, newly tarmacked horseshoe to the terminal is like a racetrack. You can pull up at speed, park anywhere and peer through the glass to see the deserted check-in desks, stationary luggage carousels and empty shells of duty-free shops. Each month, the upkeep of Berlin's ghost airport is said to cost the taxpayer €16 million. At the time of writing, it has now stood empty for almost 50 months.

On the slip road outside, new signs point to future business parks. A Total garage immediately adjoining the empty airport was well fitted out. The staff were happy to see a customer buying petrol and served me coffee and a Bratwurst. Since they were bored silly, they were happy to chat too – the garage has been open 36 months and the staff are itching to be transferred to somewhere where human beings visit. The empty Total is partnered with an empty Burger King, also staffed by a listless-looking skeleton crew.

Business on the BER site crawls along in first gear. The Holiday Inn is open and the staff rent rooms cheaply to attract some occupation to cover costs. To generate a dribble of parking income, shuttle buses run passengers from BER to Schönefeld since, ironically, the low-cost airport's car park is overfilled and chaotic while there are 10,000 almost-empty spaces at BER. As I returned my hire car to the busy Avis office at Schönefeld, the man at the desk told me, with a tone of grim satisfaction, that the BER will never open.

Over 1,500 days since BER was completed, Berlin has two temporary airports (Tegel and Schönefeld) bursting at the seams and a long-term one that has not come out of the wrapping. This is in the context of a city experiencing a tourist boom and needing ever more air travel capacity. Berliners joke darkly that they have three airports in their city – and none of them work.

Following a deadly fireball at Düsseldorf Airport in 1996, stricter fire protection regulations were the initial problem preventing the completed airport opening to the public on schedule in May 2012. Today, with Tegel and Schönefeld overfull, the situation is even more complex. Having displaced an entire village and swallowed up over €5 billion of taxes, the big issue is that the gleaming new airport is – already – not large enough and no politician has had the courage to hit the start button.

At the time of writing, no timescale has been announced that anyone really believes. Most of the taxpayers' money spent on BER today is on defending the actions of the past with expensive lawyers. The opening of BER, if it happens, and the closure of Tegel will shape the city's future and the next thousand days in Berlin.

11 WEIRD BERLIN – A TALE OF THE UNEXPECTED

IN Peter Schneider's recent book *Berlin Now*, he captures the essence of Berlin in describing its "weirdness, outlandishness, incompleteness". The author, who has lived in Berlin since 1960, stresses the energy inherent in these qualities. In my own time living and working in west Germany and in Berlin, I saw an energetic country full of surprises and paradoxes. This concluding section is something of a tale of the unexpected, pulling together many of Berlin's oddities – historical, geographical, political and social.

To the outsider, what is missing in the city can be surprising: Berlin has no springtime, no autumn, no Plaza Mayor as in central Madrid or Munich, no 700-year cathedral like Cologne or Milan, no business district like London or Paris and not a single headquarters of a major listed international company. Until recently, Berlin had very little private sector business at all. Clifford Chance, by way of example, closed its office in the city ten years ago because there were not enough businesses to generate their fees. What is missing in Berlin may be as telling as what is actually there.

Geographically, there are common misconceptions about Germany and Berlin's place in it. Many outsiders assume that Berlin is in the geographical heart of the country when, in fact, it sits as far to the east as the Czech Republic. Berlin is unmistakeably part of *Mitteleuropa* – and the city's hot/cold central European weather reflects that. The federal nature of the country is also widely misunderstood outside Germany. It is little appreciated that a deliberate decentralisation emasculated Berlin and spread economic power between Hamburg, Frankfurt, Stuttgart, Cologne, Düsseldorf and Munich.

Politically, people know about the 1990 East-West reunification which forms the backdrop to this book, but most Europeans remain unaware that Germany is a collection of fragmented cultures with no long and unified history. Unlike France or the United Kingdom, the country was not unified until 1871 when Prussian Berlin became the capital. After two world wars, the Allies sought to tone down German national identity and deselected Berlin as the capital of the *Bundesrepublik*. The feelgood factor generated by recent football World Cup tournaments has helped glue back together a federal and increasingly multicultural nation. It is only very recently (perhaps even since it successfully hosted the football World Cup in 2006) that Germany has started to regain a sense of national identity and come to terms with itself and with its past.

Financially, too, outsiders have false assumptions and do not expect Berlin to be so poor. Angela Merkel may govern Germany from her office there, but the city remains a financial backwater.

Historically, there are further surprises behind many of the standard East/West perceptions. Communist East Germany was not all negative – behind the images of the Trabants, goose-stepping jackboots and the Stasi, intelligent and talented people were bringing up families there. Many of those individuals had a feeling of fulfilment and are now missing the sense of the collective, of teamwork and of simply having a secure place to work. The recent rise in what has been termed *Ostalgie* is driven by more than patronising curiosity. Most images of the *Deutsche Demokratische Republik* appear in black and white but in researching this book, I found it unusually enlightening to look at photographs of old East Germany – usually in grainy colour. As when perusing images of the 1940s, a little colour triggers different switches in the mind. It makes it easier to empathise with real people chatting about a football match, sharing a menthol cigarette or putting a comforting arm around the shoulder of a friend.

Demographically, the Wall had some surprising benefits. Millions of talented people leaked away from the *neue Bundesländer* once it came down and in now-broken towns like Wittenberge, *die Mauer* prevented a massive 'brain drain' and emigration to the cities. The Wall helped spread jobs more evenly around the countryside. The Wittenbergers who made Veritas sewing machines had a sense of self-respect and pride in their work, even if it was poorly paid and artificial in a world where the laws of supply and demand had been suspended.

The east Berlin where I once worked was full of curious paradoxes. The attractive sandstone facade of Unter den Linden 12 masked war-damaged ruins at the back of the building. The Communist regime provided for the long-term collective good but, in the short term, recklessly dumped pollution and sewage on open fields.

To many outsiders, the other East v West surprise is the extent to which West Berlin was smoking economic dope. President Reagan may have taunted Mr Gorbachev with the bright lights and well stocked shops of the Ku'Damm, but when the state subsidies were wound down in 1995, it became clear to what degree the city had been dependent on monetary morphine. The detox was long and painful.

There are unexpected paradoxes in Berliners' behaviour. The long-running tension between Prussian *Ordnung* and the creative energy of Berlin creates polar opposites in how people interact on a daily basis. On the one hand, this means behaviour by numbers as defined in the *Bürgerliches Gesetzbuch*, the Stasi's carefully drilled and neatly labelled spyholes and an obsession with parking straight at the supermarket. On the other, it means the anarchic exuberance of the Love Parade, the sockless notary in his grand office library and the MIG fighter parked at a jaunty angle in the garden of the Tacheles squat. On the one hand, there is a widespread avoidance of first names and a default to addressing people, in speech and writing, in the formal *Sie* form. On the other, there are mixed gender showers in squash clubs and the relaxed nude barbecues on the grass in the Tiergarten.

Socially, both Germans and Berliners are also full of contradictions and surprises. Where outsiders assume they will find cold and humourless behaviour, Liz and I discovered an intriguing contrast between public and private Germans. 'The Germans' in the intimidating collective felt different from individual Germans who were amusing and very warm and have remained good friends for a long time since. Berliners absolutely have a sense of humour too, even if it is sometimes dry. Residents from Munich or Stuttgart single out the sardonic Berliner *Schnauze* (literally "snout" or big mouth) as a defining Berlin characteristic. During and after the war, the *Schnauze* provided much-needed humour in Berlin's hardest times. Today's airports and politicians are now the target of that same dark irony.

Berlin's property industry is another unexpected tale. Outsiders consistently assume that the German real estate world is a perfectly calibrated example of German engineering. In fact, the property vehicle of the Berlin pioneers was much more a Trabant than a Mercedes. Even now, the reality is that London and Paris are well-oiled international transparent markets, whilst fragmented and domestic-dominated Germany is an inefficient mess of a property industry. Berlin in the early 1990s did not even have a business community, let alone a property profession with formal training, so the construction sector was a natural magnet for the *Betonmafia* as well as the higher-profile Russian underworld.

That shadow of corruption in construction has not completely disappeared – the recent fiasco of the BER airport's non-opening is still tainted by accusations of insider dealings with contractors. The bizarre story of the BER airport is today's biggest tale of the unexpected. Outsiders are surprised that Germans would spend 15 years and over €5 billion on an empty airport – especially in the capital city of a country which likes to give lessons to Greece on austerity and corporate governance. The BER is the pinnacle of weird Berlin.

Berlin's public sector is unusually clumsy, maladministered and insolvent. It may be a legacy of the city's past that business tends to succeed in Berlin despite administration and not because of it. Two generations of Berliners grew up with no real business community experience because the West was taking dope (mainly monetary) and the East had abolished trade. After reunification, staffing local authorities was a major challenge which therefore needed reinforcements by *Zugezogene* from other parts of the country. The arrival of the apparatus of central government in 1999 failed to stimulate the private sector, so that the first part of the journey from the pioneering days was very difficult. The recent impetus of growth comes from the city's young and creative human capital rather than the *Ordnung* of middle-aged administrators.

In my short time in Berlin, I experienced a unique sense of wonder and boundless energy. It felt as if anything could happen. With the benefit of glorious hindsight, however, all that frenzy was really just a temporary intoxication. The hangover from that huge party proved to be very long and the city has needed a lot of painkillers to recover. Today's optimistic new *Weltstadt* is built on the successful healing of the deep wounds of Berlin's history – which were still wide open at the time I lived there.

In my Thousand Days in Berlin, I was fortunate to rub shoulders with some genuine property pioneers and take part in the city's euphoric party. In retrospect, I was also fortunate in timing my departure for Paris just as Berlin's long hangover was beginning. I hope that this book has left the reader with a taste for Berlin and more tales from an earlier generation of property pioneers in Paris.

Post Script

THE JOURNEY OF THE RETAIL TORTOISE AND THE OFFICE HARE

(Article published November 2016 in Property EU's Retail Watch magazine)

THE Tale of the Retail Tortoise and the Office Hare is, of course, a real estate classic. In an investment portfolio, the two main commercial sectors naturally deliver defensive and consistent on the one hand and offensive and volatile on the other. Berlin, however, is an extreme example. This tale is the story of how the city's unique circumstances amplified these typical property behaviours during its 25-year journey since reunification.

Key events snowballed before the start of the tale. Only 90 weeks after the Wall fell in November 1989, Helmut Kohl had driven through political unification, currency unification and gained approval to move the seat of government to Berlin from Bonn. Despite the breathless momentum, *Bundeskanzler* Kohl warned that the patience of the Tortoise would be necessary. He was right – it would take a generation to successfully knit together the two Germanies.

Sprinting hare, waiting tortoise – 1991 to 1996

The Hare built massively and speedily

Kohl's frantic political momentum was a natural springboard for the Office Hare. For a short time, as prime Berlin office rents tripled in only 18 months, a Hare had never raced faster. Then they halved over the next 18 months. As seen earlier in the book, that unprecedented volatility was a personal learning experience for me. Howard Ronson wrote us a pithy three-point fax explaining why offices would not make money in Berlin any time soon. "Too much land, too little business, too far from a financial hub," he declared. Howard was, characteristically, spot on.

With noise, dust, building starts and traffic jams, the Office Hare built massively and speedily. Nearly all that office construction work completed at the same time.Between 1994 and 1996, there was almost no occupier demand and for years the rebuilt Friedrichstraße in Mitte remained a ghost town. After that mad dash, the exhausted Hare fell fast asleep.

In the meantime, the Retail Tortoise peeked out from under his shell and started to consider the road ahead. Back then, it did not seem likely that the Tortoise would outpace the Hare and it is useful for today's reader to remember why this was so.

The Tortoise considered the road ahead

Retail in East Berlin had not really existed. As a student in 1988, I had crossed over to Communist Berlin for the day, dutifully changing the DM 25 (€13) into local currency. Those 25 Ostmarks proved impossible to spend. There was, simply, almost nothing to buy – other than Marxist literature and stylised posters vaunting Soviet culture. The awful food ("Hawaii Toast" and lukewarm Vita Cola) cost a few pfennigs. At reunification, some Easterners felt nauseous when first presented with a choice of fresh apples in a simple Aldi supermarket. Some had waited 15 years for a two-stroke plastic Trabant car. East Germans had procured rather than shopped.

In early 1990s west Berlin, retail also felt like procurement. Cash was king and few stores accepted or recognised credit cards – assuming they were open. Between noon on Saturday and 9am on Monday, Berlin shopping was mainly restricted to milk, bread and cheap flowers at the petrol filling station. In 1987,

Hammerson purchased prime Hertie retail redevelopment sites in Essen, Bremen and Nuremberg. Hertie's Berlin store, with its huge frontage to the Ku'damm, was rejected because, patently, west Berlin was 'never going anywhere'.

The enlarged 1990s catchment comprised subsidised West Berliners, economically uncompetitive East Berliners and impoverished East Germans on the farms around Berlin. In that context, most investors, developers and agents felt that life was too short for retail development in Berlin and ignored the sector in favour of the swifter profits in offices, residential or industrial. In 1991, with little disposable income and few places to spend it, Berlin was the retail 'sick man' of Germany.

Sleeping hare, plodding tortoise: 1996 – 2006

The long journey of the Retail Tortoise to catch the now-sleeping Hare was slowed by major headwinds. Firstly, Berlin subsidies were wound down from 1995, making poorer, grumpier west Berliners. Then, for over a decade, multiple taxes were levied to pay for east Germany's jobs, drains, phones and trains.

The Tortoise plods through strong headwinds

From 1995, talented young people began to move out of Berlin to live in happier places with happier prospects. Between 1949 and 1961, the DDR leaked 2.7 million citizens – for the same reasons. Now that there was no longer a wall to keep people in, the former DDR would lose a further 2.7 million. That started a long, long decline in residential values until, near the bottom of Berlin's downturn in 2007, inflation-adjusted house prices were much lower than in the 1970s. Tenant-friendly legislation discouraged residential landlords from investing money and apartments stayed empty, graffiti-ridden and unloved.

By 2006, Berlin had become a unique property market outlier – physically and financially. Where debt finance had driven values up around Europe, prices had largely floated downwards in Berlin. Former mayor Klaus Wowereit coined the famous description of Berlin as "poor but sexy".

Those falling residential values were also a fair barometer of the consumer spending mood. Many years after reunification, there was, very tangibly, not a lot of money in a still-wounded Berlin.

The healing of Berlin's wounds: 2007 – 2016

So what changed? Many fundamentals gradually healed the deep and painful wounds of Berlin and in doing so, opened up the path for our Retail Tortoise:

1) Economics: Gerhard Schröder's government cracked the entitlement culture in the early 2000s, leaving Angela Merkel to harvest the benefits years later.

2) Politics: Merkel, herself a long term political Tortoise (and from the Berlin/Brandenburg area), has demonstrated credibility and stability.

3) Infrastructure: The seeds of new infrastructure have produced shoots of optimism in Berlin consumer sentiment. The new airport is still not yet open, but since 2006, the five-level main train station *Hauptbahnhof* has helped consolidate a polycentric city.

4) World Cup 2006: That station had been opened for the 2006 football World Cup, which Germany hosted. The well-staged tournament was a tangible retail turning point – as Berliners on the *Fanmeile* once more felt proud to be German.

5) Tourism: Berlin leapfrogged Rome to become the third tourist city in Europe behind London and Paris. In the post-2008 global financial crisis period, both business and leisure tourists have boosted retail sales in a very affordable city.

6) Privatisation: Privatising the residential sector and improving the quality of living space has contributed to the long-term success of retail.

7) Demographics: The 'brain drain' has been reversed – a major stimulus of retail success. Berlin was once again perceived as a great place to live and has remained a vibrant party city for the young and energetic.

8) Business: In the 1990s, not a single DAX company was headquartered in Berlin. Since 2008, Berlin has become a business start-up hub with growing organisations like Zalando and SoundCloud.

The victorious retail tortoise – 2016

The overriding feeling in the city today is optimism. Easterners, Westerners, tourists and the many *Zugezogene* (Germans who have moved from outside Berlin) mostly see the future in a good light.

While Germany as a whole is forecast to shrink, Berlin's demographics are strong, even excluding 'migrant' growth. Each week, over 1,000 new Berliners arrive in the city. By 2030, the capital is forecast to have a population of 4 million, taking it back to the size of the 1920s 'golden age'.

Gentrification is radiating out from the historical centre of gravity of Berlin Mitte. In East Berlin, Pankow's sleek, noiseless trams have replaced the clanking Communist-era rolling stock, while Prenzlauer Berg is famously home to the *Prenzlschwäbin* ('yummy mummies' from wealthy Stuttgart). In the former West, Neukoelln and Kreuzberg are today's fast-evolving districts where graffiti can (just about) be perceived as street art. The long-running social tension between Prussian *Ordnung* and Berlin's freethinking culture has tilted in favour of the freethinking newbies of *Silicon Allee*.

Today's really powerful retail story is the much improved non-institutional street shopping. In the West, much is changing around the Zoo and with the lengthening retail pitch of the Ku'damm and refit of KaDeWe and Karstadt. In the East, cultural hub Rosenthaler Straße now offers luxury brands. Beyond these mainstream references in agents' reports, the most dynamic consumer spending is perhaps in the 24/7 cafés of Kreuzberg's Schlesische Straße and in shops and bars under railway arches – West and East. Today's citizens of Pankow, discomforted by Aldi's fruit selection a generation ago, enjoy fresh strawberry stalls next to the currywurst kiosks.

Shopping centres have been less successful than street retail. In the worst period of the tax headwinds, a UK investor's poor experience with a centre in Reinickendorf still serves as a cautionary tale. Even if Berlin's tough winter climate favours shopping under cover, the stock lacks the 'wow factor' – with the possible exception of the new 300-store Mall of Berlin, a non-replicable urban mega centre developed by Dr Huth, himself a hard-to-replicate entrepreneur, unusual on the stage of world class retail.

The 'European Champions League' of shopping centre players such as ECE, Sonae and MFI Unibail serve much the same offering as in Hamburg, Warsaw and Prague (plus a few *Ampelmann* shops for a splash of local colour). The recently refurbished Bikini Haus at Bahnhof Zoo is more innovative, a mixed-use building with some pop-up shops amid the cool merchandising. The Bikini's unique 'wow factor' is to create a sense of place with the popular Monkey Bar, which overlooks the Zoo's animals from the tenth floor of its boutique hotel.

Retail risks and downsides remain. Berlin's spending power is still 50% lower than Munich's and the city is oversupplied with shopping centres – with still more under construction. By the steady standards of real estate Germany, optimistic Berlin could prove volatile. Zalando is an example of a major employer with a fragile business model and strong growth.

By almost any measure, the Retail Tortoise has outrun the Office Hare.

Over a generation since the start of our tale in 1991, rental growth in prime shops has proved much stronger than offices. Prime shop rents have almost doubled since 2006, whilst prime office rents are still below late 1994 levels (when I left Berlin).

The best part of the story is wealth distribution. In 2015, the former DDR states finally posted the same economic growth rate as west Germany. To put that huge achievement in context, consider parallels with South Africa. Either side of New Year 1989/90, the certainties of the protected systems of Communism and Apartheid were unexpectedly cracked wide open. Whilst Johannesburg will need yet another generation to bloom, the grassroots retail story is already flourishing in Berlin.

In the end, Howard Ronson and Helmut Kohl were both right – it did, indeed, take a generation. Coincidentally, Angela Merkel was Kohl's East German protegée. She grew up speaking Russian in the Brandenburg countryside outside Berlin and, like the Tortoise, Frau Merkel has proved the value of progressing to the winning line at a measured pace.

And the Retail Tortoise? He was so far ahead of the Hare that there was even time to raise a family of energetic East German retail youngsters, fit and ready for the challenges of Germany's next 25 years.

Glossary of German Language Expressions

Alltag	Day-to-day routine
Altlasten	pollution (literally 'old burdens')
Altstadt	old town
der Ampelmann	red/green walking character on ex-DDR traffic lights
Asylantenheim	refugee home
Atomschutzbunker	underground nuclear shelter
Baubeamte des Senats	senior planning official of Berlin Senate
Baulücke	Infill site for development – literally "building hole"
Bebauungsplan (or B-Plan)	Zoning Plan – outline level of permission in planning process
BER	International flight code for new Berlin Brandenburg airport
Besatzungsmächte	the four occupying powers in Berlin – USA, France, UK, USSR
Betonmafia	"concrete mafia" – closed circle of West Berlin contractors
Bundesrepublik	Federal Republic of Germany (West Germany)
Bürgerliches Gesetzbuch (BGB)	Federal Law Book
Deutsche Demokratische Republik (DDR)	German Democratic Republic (GDR) – East Germany
die Wende	'the turning' – generic expression for changes through reunification
Eintritt	entrance fee
Endstation	final or terminus station of bus or rail journey
Ersatz	literally 'replacement' – often used in wartime Germany
Fanmeile	the long World Cup 'Fan Zone' along the Straße 17 Juni

Gasthaus	public house
Geisterbahnhof	abandoned station (especially in no-man's land during Cold War)
Gewerbepark	high-density German-style business park
Großflughafen	major airport – especially of BER
Grundsteinlegung	groundbreaking ceremony prior to construction
Güterverkehrszentrum (GVZ)	freight centre
Hauptbahnhof	central train station
Haus der Ministerien	Ministries Building (in DDR)
Hausmeister(-in)	concierge
Haussmannian	Architectural style in Paris – often in residential use
Hausverwaltung	property management
Hertie	former West German chain of department stores
Hinterhof	rear courtyard – a distinctive Berlin style of architecture
Internationales Handelszentrum (IHZ)	the high-rise World Trade Center of East Berlin
kalter Krieg	Cold War
Kleinmoskau	"little Moscow" – nickname of Wünsdorf in Brandenburg
Makler/Immobilienmakler	broker/property broker
Mehrwegflasche	recyclable bottle
mietfreie Zeit	rent-free period
Mitte	one of the administrative districts of central Berlin
Mitteleuropa	Central Europe
Musterraum	showsuite for letting offices
neue Bundesländer (NBL)	the five new federal states of former East Germany
Ostalgie	nostalgia for the culture of former East Germany
Rathaus	town hall
Rieselfelder	sewage fields in DDR

Sächsische Schweiz	low-lying mountain range near the German/Czech border
Scheunenviertel	old Jewish Quarter in Mitte (literally 'Barn Quarter')
Schicki Micki	Yuppie/Flash Harry
Schloss	former palace building of Hohenzollern Royal Family
Schnauze	'Snout' – especially referring to Berlin's sardonic sense of humour
Schneeregen	sleet
Siezen	to address people in the formal and polite 'Sie' form
Silicon Allee	location of Berlin's technological industries
Staatsbibliothek	national library building on Unter den Linden
Staatssicherheitsdienst (Stasi)	East German secret police
SXF	International flight code for Schönefeld airport
Treuhandanstalt (THA)	liquidator of state-owned assets in former East Germany
TXL	International flight code for Tegel airport
Verkehrskreiseln	roundabouts
Vita Cola	brand of cola in former East Germany
Volkspalast	Former DDR's cultural centre on Alexanderplatz
Waldbühne	Open-air amphitheatre for concerts near Olympic Stadium
Wasser-zweckverband	water company
Weltstadt	world city
Wiedervereinigung	reunification
Zeitgeist	spirit of the age
Zersetzung	mental disintegration
Zugezogene	Berlin residents originating from outside the city

Aerial Photographs (2016)

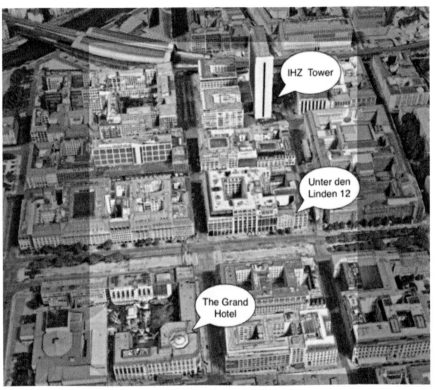

CENTRAL EAST BERLIN
Friedrichstraße and Unter den Linden
The former Weatherall Green and Smith office at Unter den Linden 12,
located between two iconic landmarks of the former DDR – The Grand Hotel and
the tower of the Internationales Handelszentrum (IHZ) on Friedrichstraße

BERLIN LICHTENBERG

Normannenstraße – The rectangular buildings of the former Stasi HQ and Berlin Lichtenberg

BRANDENBURG PARK

The village of Genshagen adjoining Brandenburg Park and its Coca-Cola buildings
The A10 Berliner Ring runs along the south of the park

Maps

Map 1. Central East Berlin

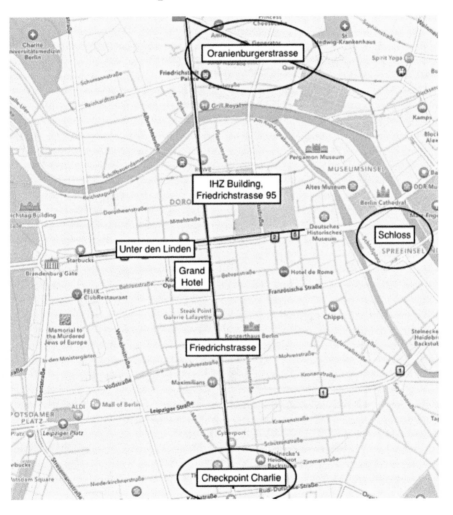

Map 2. Central West Berlin

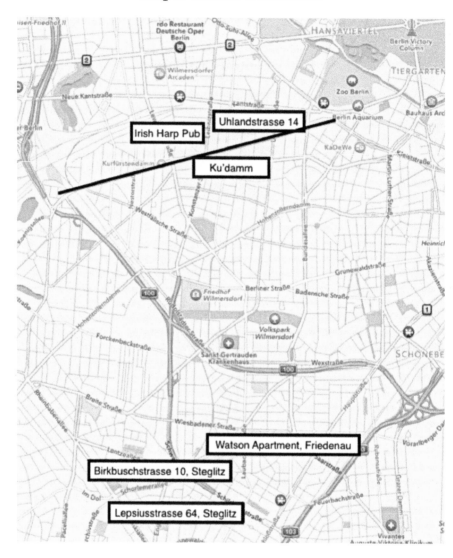

Map 3. Neue Bundesländer – Former DDR

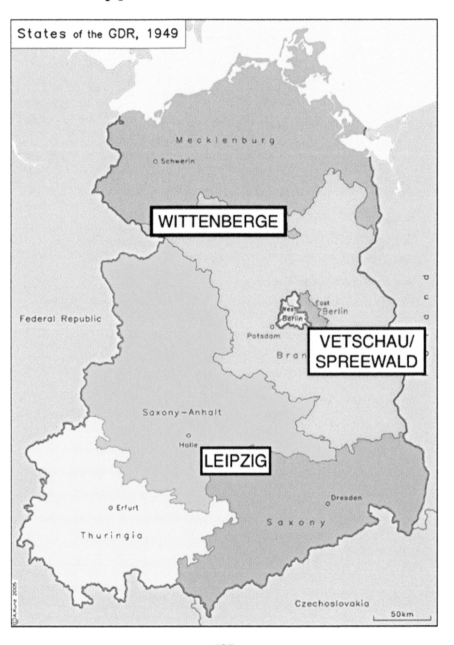

States of the GDR, 1949

Mecklenburg

o Schwerin

WITTENBERGE

Federal Republic

East Berlin

West Berlin

o Potsdam

Bran

VETSCHAU/ SPREEWALD

Saxony-Anhalt

o Halle

LEIPZIG

o Dresden

Saxony

o Erfurt

Thuringia

Czechoslovakia

50km

Map 4. Southern Berliner Ring

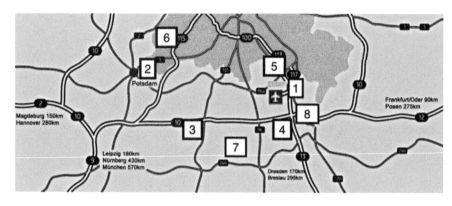

Key to Map

1. Flughafen Schönefeld
2. Potsdam
3. Brandenburg Park, Genshagen
4. Königspark, Königs Wusterhausen

5. Future Flughafen (BER)
6. Europarc, Dreilinden
7. Wünsdorf
8. A10 Einkaufszentrum, Wildau

Acknowledgements

I would like to acknowledge the many people who helped me in producing this book.

In the first place, my thanks to those living in Berlin today who welcomed me back and whose 'then and now' perspective was instructive and energising – Busso, Barbara, Harry, Markus and Martin. Particular thanks to Stuart Reid for Rockspring's sponsorship and agreeing to write his '10,000 Days in Berlin' foreword.

Many 'ex-Berliners' assisted me with their vivid memories of that exceptional time. I am grateful to those who helped recall the moment: Batty, Gillum, Richards, Duckworth, Cruicky, Corky, Fraser, Mich, Marc, Michael Spies and Michael Badger. Special thanks to my former client Philip Jones for opening his scrapbook and taking the time to reflect on the detail of the Horsham/Coca-Cola story.

I am indebted to contributors who did not live in Berlin but lived or worked in Germany: Tim, Henry, David, Olly, Hannelore, Anthony and Adam O in Canada for his memories of our 1988 excursion to Berlin as students. Posthumous thanks to the late Chris Bull-Diamond who insisted, as he would have done half a life ago, that this was an important piece of work and needed to be done to the very best of my ability.

A particular acknowledgement to former colleague Fabian Münster for his originality and skilled architect's eye with the graphics. I am also indebted to Ray for the graphic design, Cristina and my son Ali Watson for their assistance with visuals.

I would like to acknowledge my editor, Gordon Darroch, for his judicious and culturally-perceptive shaping of the text and his toning down of my odd habit of capitalising nouns – as if writing in German. There are many fewer Capital Letters now. Thanks also to the many proofreaders amongst my friends and family; Clare, Aoife, Steph, my wife Liz, father-in-law Harold, son Christopher and brother Steve, who encouraged me whilst I was writing this at his home in New Zealand.

I have been fortunate to have professional guidance from Sophie and Véronique and, above all, Judi Seebus, Spiritual Godmother of this project who guided me towards recognising the importance of an authentic narrative voice. Thanks to all of you for helping me launch this creative adventure.

References

My own memory has been the main source of material in this book. The people previously acknowledged have greatly helped me in this since my recall is, of course, no longer as certain as during the thousand days. In addition, I have enjoyed reading around the subject to verify certain assumptions and facts. The following were useful references to me:

Articles:

Berlin: A Profile – LSE cities – (Jens Bisky) 2006

European Cities Planning Systems and Property Markets – (Berry, McGreal) 2004

Wünsdorf – a cold war ruin but with potential (New York Times) 1995

Coca-Cola (Fortune) Coca-Cola's Berlin Wall lessons in leadership 2009

Coca-Cola – (Bloomberg) the real thing is thundering eastward 1992

Urban planning without Vision in Berlin (der Spiegel online) 2013

Market Reports/Statistical:

Bundesamt – Deutscher Bundestag – bundestag.de – re Autobahn statistics East v West in 1992

TLG market report 2015 – Immobilienstandorte in Ostdeutschland

Bulwien Gasa 1975 – 2004

Berlin Housing – (Piet Eichholz) 2008

Amt für Statistik – article in Berliner Morgenpost June 2015 re Zugezogene

Videos:

Berlin – 3 part documentary series BBC – (Matt Frei) 2009

The dark secrets of a surveillance state – TED talk – (Hubertus Knabe)

Pepsi v Coke in the Ice Cold War – (John Pilger)

Books:

Berlin Now –The Rise of the City and the Fall of the Wall (Peter Schneider) 2014

The File (Timothy Garton-Ash) 1997

1989 The Berlin Wall – My part in its downfall (Peter Millar) 2009

Stasiland – Stories from Behind the Berlin Wall (Anna Funder) 2001

Poor but Sexy – Culture Clashes in Europe East and West (Agata Pyzik) 2014

Chambers Book of Great Speeches (for Ronald Reagan in Berlin 1987)

DDR in Color (Klaus Morgenstern) 2013

Websites/Photographic:

Berliner Zeitung Archiv http://www.berliner-zeitung.de/archiv

Berliner Morgenpost Archiv http://www.morgenpost.de/suche/

Stadt Berlin – official plans site: http://fbinter.stadt-berlin.de/fb/index

Berlin airport BER berlin-airport.de

Abandoned Berlin http://www.abandonedberlin.com/p/map.html

Stadt Ludwigsfelde www.ludwigsfelde.de

Michael Lange Tumblr 90er – photographs http://90erberlin.tumblr.com/

Gerd Danigel – Deutsche Fotothek – http://www.deutschefotothek.de/

Berlin Wonderland – http://interaktiv.morgenpost.de/wonderland/